SCHOOL Me

How to Help Your Kid Dominate the School Year without Losing It

Bishonna Jones

BJ LEGACIES
Unlimited
Education | Media | Family

Printed in the United States of America
ISBN Paperback: 978-0-692-15137-2

DEDICATION

In Memory of Linda Faye Jones who promoted both
education and family. Well Done.

May 16, 1950 – October 29, 2018
Rest In Heaven Mama

TABLE OF CONTENTS

TIME TO GET SCHOOLED!

W ORLD DOMINATION-- that's it. That's the desire that we have for our children. Over these 15 years in education, I've come to realize that while we all may look, speak, worship, and love differently, we still want the same basics for our kids. We want them to be H2S2: Healthy, Happy, Safe, and Successful. Now while we all have that desire, many come to the school unsure of how to do it. Most parents have heard that in order to help kids succeed in school you must make sure they read daily. We get it. Start reading. But besides that, we're often not sure of next steps. Parenting is tough and getting our children to do their best and be their best is no small feat. However, I can help. While there are plenty of things I completely suck at (never ask me to do a 5K with you...you've been warned) helping parents survive grades K-12 while building stronger families isn't one of them. Supporting parents is my passion and I have completely geeked out over the research and have a pre-teen fanatic attachment to the mission of family engagement. Let's just say I have learned some things that can help us out tremendously while trying to support our children in school. I have discovered information that makes being an engaged parent actually doable.

The Book and You

After working with countless parents, I began to notice a pattern. Most parents had the same questions when it came to school and student success. Light bulb moment! That's when I decided to write a book that answers the 14 most commonly asked questions from parents regarding supporting our children at school. This literary work was created to be a quick go-to guide of best practices and invaluable information to encourage our children's academic success and more consistent engagement at home. Is the book all-inclusive, and does it cover everything that happens at your child's school? No. Now I have confidence in my abilities, but to cover everything that happens at every school in the country is pretty impossible. The purpose of this book is to give a snapshot of the topics and to spark both conversation and action. What we will do is cover basics that are common at most K-12 institutions that will help you gain clarity and save tons of time, energy, and stress. Less stressed parents lead to less stressed kids who will in turn create a fantabulous school year and happier homes. Please note that in this book, "parent" refers to those with a dominant role in the child's life. In this book "parent" represents biological parents as well as guardians and other caretakers.

The Structure

The book is organized into chapters and each chapter contains three parts: table talk, tips and strategies, and an affirmation. *Table Talk* is where we break down the focus question or questions. The *Messenger Tips* section is where I share best practices and advice. *Affirmations* are an opportunity for us to speak power over ourselves, children, and the school year. I'm a firm believer in speaking what you want into existence, so positivity is a must. Another thing to note is that each chapter discusses a standalone topic and therefore can be read in any order and not necessarily chronological. Think of your priorities and start with the chapter question that most closely matches your top one.

Now that we are all caught up to speed, are you ready? Ready to get some questions answered and confusion cleared? Ready to help your kid dominate the school year without losing it? Are you ready to get schooled?

CHAPTER 1

Let's Get Ready to Rumble

QUESTION 1: HOW SHOULD WE PREPARE FOR THE NEW SCHOOL YEAR?

Right before school starts parents seriously consider a lock for the refrigerator. The temperature is still high, the kids are still hungry, and the commercials of smiling faces with cool hair, new sneakers, and crayons are starting to show more frequently. You got it. It's Back-to-School Time! Depending on where you fall in this triangular relationship of student-parent-educator, emotions may vary. One thing is for sure, it's coming and being ready is a must. Here are some key things every parent should do when preparing for the new school year.

Summer Wind Down

Summers are made for relaxing and memory making with a few academic endeavors tossed in for balance. With this being said, don't end the summer abruptly. Still make room for downtime and fun. A last rendezvous at the beach, waterpark, hiking trail, or theme park may be just what the doctor ordered before the business of a new school year begins. Just like some days we simply don't feel like adulting, kids feel the same. An unplanned day is often the best kind of day, so make sure to allow for those too. The last thing anyone wants is to start the school year off agitated and stressed because you're tired from all the "summer work."

Routines

To lessen the stress of a new school year, implement a back-to-school routine 2-3 weeks prior to the start date. A back-to-school routine would be the actions that you take consistently every year before the start of a new school year. This may include sending the kids to bed and waking them earlier than their summer norm, ending use of electronics at a specified time, or resuming their everyday school year chores a few weeks before school starts. These routines are important because they give their bodies and mind a chance to adjust to the expectations abandoned during summer break. If you want to keep peace in the house, it's best to introduce each adjustment gradually than to expect kids to go from 0 to 100 in two seconds flat.

Registration

Does your child's school require that you register every year? If so, use summer break to do it. The closer you wait to the start of the school year, the longer the registration lines will be. Can you complete registration online? Does the school have your most recent information for home and work? If you've moved since the end of the previous school year, make sure to have evidence of residency including mortgage papers or leasing contracts. Also, be sure to have documentation of any special parental custody arrangements. Be sure the legal documents outline the specifics of any restrictions because your word alone won't do. Do you have access to birth certificates and school records (or last semester's report card)? It's important to keep those documents handy. Visit the school's website for a complete list of requirements.

Health Checks

Summer is the perfect time for that dentist or doctor visit since summer schedules are more flexible. Something to keep on your radar are immunizations and rescue medication. Updated immunizations are usually a requirement when entering kindergarten and 7th grade. Most schools have a grace period to get it done, but it is best to handle prior to school starting to avoid the child being withdrawn later and missing days of instruction. If you are exempt from immunizations, prepare to provide the necessary information for school documentation purposes. For students with chronic illnesses needing medication during the school day, be sure to have unexpired medicine in its original container (prescriptions should have the student's name on the label) available for the nurse. If the child is old enough to self-administer medicine, make sure to review the process before school starts and double check the school's disbursement of medicine policy. Many schools require a student to take medicine in the presence of an adult even if they are able to do it themselves. Does your child play sports at the school level? Don't forget about the sports physical. Most are valid for a one-year period only and if you need a new one summer is perfect for getting it.

Summer Assignments

Another item on the back-to-school checklist is the often overlooked summer assignments. Many schools have a mandatory summer reading list that must be completed before the first day along with other accompanying tasks. These assignments are usually the first grades entered for the new year. The last thing a parent wants to discover a week before school starts is that their child has 5 books to read in 5 days. And the last thing a student wants to do is begin the school year with zeros in the gradebook. Not sure if your kid has summer work? Check the school's website for info. Something as important as this is usually featured on the school's homepage. Summer reading lists are an excellent way to combat the dreadful summer slide, which is the experience of students losing academic skills in reading and math during the summer months. It is not uncommon for students to lose two months of reading and over 2.5 months of math skills in one summer. This is why it is so important to make sure our kids are reading at least 30 minutes a day and practicing their acquired math skills over the break. If not recouped, the loss of skills accumulates each summer. Before you know it, our kids could easily be grade levels behind in reading and math. Double check the school's website for summer assignment information. If no assignments are due, assign work of your own for practice.

School Supply Lists

Time for the infamous back-to-school shopping list. First let me divulge this truth. Everything on the list is not necessarily needed. Teachers operate on the "it's best to have and not need, than to need and not have" system. However, I will say that it's smart to buy the 48 #2 pencils, 6 packs of wide ruled notebook paper, and 10 dry erase markers now while things are dirt cheap than to wait until two months down the road when everything has tripled in price. For upper grade levels, wait to buy the big ticket items until after the first class. Often those items are *suggestions* and not mandatory unless noted on the list as "mandatory." If they are truly necessary, the teacher will reiterate that during their first class. I'm sure some moms are clutching their pearls at this information, BUT while I don't know everything, experience has found this to be 9 out of 10 times true. While everything on the list is not usually needed, that is not an excuse for a child to be ill-prepared. Every student will need basics like paper, folders, writing utensils, and something to haul it all in at a minimum. Teachers will provide an updated supply list at Open House.

Reflections, Expectations, and Projections

Okay. So we have taken our last summer vacation, registered the kids for school, started our daily routines, did the health checks and summer assignments, plus tackled the back-to-school shopping list. What else could there possibly be left to do? Three words for you: Reflections- Expectations- Projections. How this looks at your house will depend on the culture of your family. I tend to be over the top and exaggerate EVERYTHING so this piece can get fancy. What I need you, the parent, to do is this...talk. I need you to speak to your child about the previous school year (Reflection). We need to discuss what went right, what went wrong, what we want to do more of and what needs to happen less. Basically discuss the highlights and lowlights. Next, I need you to verbalize your expectations for your child and the upcoming year. You will need to provide a *why* for each expectation. Relevance is key to building relationships and making expectations stick. Kids don't do things because we tell them to, they oblige when they respect the relationship we have with them. So be completely transparent here and let your heart lead the conversation. I try to include academic, social, and emotional expectations because I need my kids to be well-rounded and grounded and not just scholars. Lastly, let the kids make goals for themselves (Projections). What is it that they want to accomplish this year? A few goals are all it takes. I suggest no more than 4 goals and for them to be a variety of academic, social, and emotional. What's important here is focus. Now for the fun part, make a visual representation of the goals. A visual helps us remember what it is that we seek to accomplish. One year I posted our school year goals on a big dry-erase board in the hallway. Every morning we had to walk pass the board and it served as a reminder to stay the course. We would have goal talks too to check on the progress of the family and to see what adjustments should be made. The kids enjoyed it and felt a sense of accomplishment as they were able to check goals off the list as…DONE! Visuals are great tools to assist with accountability and the earlier we teach kids to be accountable for their actions the better.

Now for the extras…

-----Messenger Tips-----

- Use the back-to-school specials to stock up on basic supplies like paper, pens, pencils, folders, and crayons to keep at home. Send to school as needed.

- Buy a few poster boards now to keep on hand for projects later.

- Designate an area for homework and keep supplies and resource materials (dictionary, thesaurus, tablet/laptop) handy for quick access.

- Spruce up the house. Switch the furniture around, change the sheets, declutter, or maybe add a fresh scent plugin. The idea of out with the old and in with the new translates well to fresh starts and a new school year.

- Have the child plan outfits for the first week of school. This will keep stress down in the morning and lessen the chance of your child going to school frantic, mismatched, and wrinkled.

- Take care of lunch. If they take lunch to school, make sure to organize items for a quick grab and go. If they buy lunch, make sure to add money to their account before the first day of school. Most schools

offer online systems to add money to lunch accounts.
You can also check the online account to see if there
is money available from the previous school year.

I WILL HELP MY KID DOMINATE THE SCHOOL YEAR WITHOUT LOSING IT BY...

Getting a jumpstart on the year through advance preparation. I will not wait until the last minute to practice routines, register for school, or assist with summer assignments. The last minute rush is what causes stress. I will also allow my child to mentally prepare by giving them downtime and sharing my expectations for the upcoming year. As a family we will set goals, create visuals, and work to create the best school year yet!

CHAPTER 2

SCHOOL EVENTS

QUESTION 2: DO WE REALLY HAVE TO GO?

Are you a proactive or reactive person? When it comes to handling business, do you prefer to plan ahead or go with the flow? This is what you must keep in mind when considering school events and meetings. Do I want to know what to expect or react to it after it's happened? Also, what is the purpose of the event or meeting, and is it something I consider or should consider a priority? These are all valid questions. Now, is attendance at every school function necessary? No, but here are common school events to consider attending and why.

Open House/Meet the Teacher

The beginning of every school year usually starts with Open House. Open House is a time for the parents and students to meet the teachers, school staff, and tour the building if needed. This is also when teachers give out the supply list, briefly discuss expectations, and gather parent contact info. It's honestly a time to ease some of the stress felt by parents and students about the beginning of a new school year. Students get to see where to go on the first day of school and a sneak peek at who their classmates may be, and parents get to give the teachers a one over putting faces and names together. Teachers are responsible for much of our children's day for around 10 months out of the year. We want to be introduced to and establish a relationship with those with this kind of responsibility as early as possible. However, don't come with high hopes of learning all of the details of what will be covered in class. Those details come at a later time. This is simply a meet and greet. If it's just a greeting, why come? You want to come to Open House for many reasons with one being: it is YOUR first impression and we *always* want to make a great first impression. Please know that while we are checking out the teachers, the teachers are also checking out us! They are monitoring how their future student reacts to the parent's body language and words, how the parent articulates and interacts with them and those around them, and if the parent is being pleasant, patient , hurried, or rude. They are also making note if the parent cared enough to attend this very brief introduction or at least send someone to represent the family. That's right. The teachers aren't the only ones on display. We are too. So, attendance at Open House is a way to make an early statement about your stance and investment in your child's education.

Curriculum Night

The details that you didn't get at Open House you get now. What exactly are the students learning? How will they learn it? How will they be evaluated on it? What are the best means for communication? Open House was the appetizer. Curriculum Night equals meat and potatoes because it's a time to break down the course focus areas, standards, and goals. You may also get access to websites and other helpful resources to support the learning of the content at home. Whereas Open House was the soft greeting, Curriculum Night is when we get down to business. Think of it as a group conference night where the basics are laid out. This is when the teachers get technical. Pay close attention to the documents that are given out at this meet up. They are usually more formal and abiding than the general data collection packets given at Open House.

Parent Workshops

Because every parent needs some guidance in supporting their child's learning, there will be a variety of capacity building parent workshops offered throughout the year. What the workshops will cover depends on the needs of the school and requests of the parents. At the elementary level training in reading and math strategies are common, at the middle school level we progress to more support in the areas of technology and math (parents and this "new math" don't often mix), and high school is all about next level preparation i.e., SAT/ACT intensives, financial aid, scholarships, and college application support, or an overview on graduation requirements. These workshops are often short, sweet, and jammed full of tricks of the trade to help move your child forward. If you don't see something offered that you need, be sure to reach out to let the coordinator know. FREEZE! Who is responsible for coordinating the parent workshops for your school? This is a question EVERY parent needs to know. You have a connection in the building. There is someone there that works diligently to connect parents and the community to information and resources to support the student, and you need to know who that person is or who those people are. This information should not be top secret as the purpose of much of their responsibility is community outreach. The community can't reach you if you are not visible and wanting to be found. In Title I schools, you should ask for the person responsible for parent involvement or family engagement. In non-Title I schools multiple people may play the part depending on the training being offered. Suggestion, start off with the school counselors or the leading parent organization (PTO, PTA, & etc.). So when it comes to parent workshops, examine your gaps in development and information and attend those that address the lack thereof.

Parent Organization Functions

As soon as the words PARENT ORGANIZATION fly from the lips most automatically assume we are discussing the Parent-Teacher Association (PTA). While that is quite the reputation, that is hardly the truth. There are a variety of parent groups out there including Parent Teacher Organization (PTO), Booster Clubs, Watch D.O.G.S., and All Pro Dads just to name a few. Parent organizations have their own agendas and are usually independent of the school's governance (aside from booster clubs). The focus on specific content standards' strengths and weaknesses and ways parents can assist with such is left up to the schools to handle. After all, teachers are the experts on those matters. The parental groups tend to focus on general academic support topics and areas like technology, school culture and structure, community partnership opportunities, fundraising, parenting, and extracurricular activities. Many of the groups' purpose is a combination of student advocacy, parent involvement, and school-parent-community transparency. These groups want to make sure that the schools continue to operate in the best interest of the families they serve and use their membership for school partnering activities. Think of it this way. These groups work in conjunction with the schools as supports, but are not controlled by the schools. So if you are looking for a more independent voice about the needs and direction of the school, attending a parent organization meeting could definitely be beneficial.

Governance Meetings

School is a business. Let us not forget that. That means that there is a defined hierarchy and a mandatory system of checks and balances in place to keep the organization functioning as a legitimate institution. Unlike corporations, schools are funded by the government and the need for complete transparency is not requested but expected. Governance meetings are necessary to stay abreast of the decisions being made at the school level. Topics discussed at this time include school-wide initiatives, discipline, hires or promotions, disbursement of funds and budgets. School council meetings, principal town hall meetings, and Title I planning meetings are wonderful examples of these opportunities. It is at these meetings where you will hear about the nuts and bolts of the school and see true decision making in progress. Unfortunately, traditionally these meetings have had some of the lowest turnouts of all school events even though by far they affect the most changes. No sugarcoating this. If we want to solve the ills of the school, we have to be present with the decision makers when the conversations are being had. Period. Want to find out what's going on at the district level? Make a point of attending at least one school board meeting a year and bookmark where to find the meeting minutes for those you can't attend. Policy is presented, discussed, and amended at these meetings and public input is sought at every one. You can visit the district's website for school board meeting dates, agendas, board member profiles, and meeting minutes.

Signature Celebrations

On a lighter note every school has its signature events. Maybe it's a huge STEM (science, technology, engineering, and math) Festival, International Night, an annual community fundraiser, or homecoming. Whatever it may be, I suggest you attend at least one. The time and effort that goes into planning these events is borderline extreme, and that may be an understatement. So, just out of pure respect for the dedication of the staff you should want to support the event, but there are other perks. Most signature events are casual and fun which is a change from the more formal and structured offerings. They are opportunities to build relationships with the staff and other school families while experiencing hands on learning while working side by side (or cheering side by side) with your child. They also offer an opportunity to learn about community school partnerships and resources that may benefit your family outside of school. And let us not forget good ol' fashioned school spirit. A community that rallies behind its schools is something powerful and sought after. It's no surprise that schools with high numbers of active parents and local businesses tend to perform better, than those without that community backing (nea.org, 2008). Hey, they often have better athletic programs and competitive clubs too. It takes a village. High performing schools lead to higher property values too, so it's a win-win for everyone. Events of this magnitude don't happen frequently so advertisement starts early which gives you plenty of time to plan to attend.

Again, do we have to go to school events? That answer is up to you, but if you plan on being an involved and informed parent, it is a simple YES. Attending EVERYTHING is not necessary or expected. The goal is to be active and in the loop. To do so does not require your presence at every single event on the calendar, so be strategic. What information is most important to you and your family right now and in the immediate future? When deciding on what to attend, start with that simple question. Make those events that fulfill that void a priority, and then add others as your schedule permits. The goal of your participation at these events is capacity building. We want to build your capacity as a parent to support your child, advocate for your child, and support the school community.

------- **Messenger Tips**-------

- Mark school meetings and events on a calendar as soon as you hear about them to keep from forgetting as life gets hectic.

- Know your focus. What information do you need to know at this moment? What skills do you need to gain to help support or advocate for your child? What resources or policies could benefit your family? What are you curious about when it comes to school business?

- Prioritize multiple focuses.

- Get your child's input on what they are interested in and would like to attend.

- Don't disregard an event or meeting for fear of it being "long and boring." We know this is a common fear of parents, and we work hard to spruce things up (and keep things as short as possible but still effective). Remember, just because something isn't entertaining does not mean it's not helpful.

- Keep in mind that opportunity presents itself to people who are VISIBLE. Attending events are great for learning information and NETWORKING. Strong relationships will open up doors quicker than credentials alone. People will support you and pour resources into you (and your child) if they know that you are actively engaged in their work and mission. SHOW UP. Out of sight…out of mind.

- Schools are ALWAYS looking for leaders. Don't be afraid to run for school council, hold a leadership role in a parent organization, or lend your expertise to a signature event. We would love to have ya!

I WILL HELP MY KID DOMINATE THE SCHOOL YEAR WITHOUT LOSING IT BY...

Staying abreast of school functions and prioritizing our participation. I am well aware that I do not have to be at every event at all times to prove my involvement. I will be selective in attending the activities most beneficial to my family and will construct ways to stay informed about other opportunities. The idea is to participate smarter to acquire knowledge, build relationships, encourage school spirit, and increase the skills and capacity of myself and my child.

CHAPTER 3

Transitioning

QUESTION 3: WHAT SHOULD WE EXPECT AT THE NEXT LEVEL?

Anticipation and excitement all wound up as one is how both parents and students normally feel about grade level transitioning, and how could we blame them? It's an interesting time in a student's schooling, a milestone. The transition from preschool to elementary school, from elementary to middle school, and from middle school to high school marks the educational and personal maturity of the student on the road to total independence. Independence is an idea that some people- flirt with, but is much harder to fully embrace. Hence, the anxiousness of grade level transitioning can cause feelings of overwhelm. The thought of new responsibilities, expectations, and the unknown can be a challenging time for students and parents. Here's what we know about the process that can serve to help us all.

Preschool to Elementary School

Moving from preschool to elementary, we can expect tons of tears on the parents' part. Hey, the truth is the truth. The kids are excited and the parents are terrified. Our babies aren't so much of a baby anymore. Structurally, we can expect more of it. There is a need for the allowance of natural flow in preschool. There are plans in place, but teachers are aware of the great need for flexibility. In kindergarten, the structure becomes more rigid with fewer breaks. There is also a shift from rote memorization to more critical thinking, a greater call for accountability on the child's part, and the beginning of more shared communication between the school, student, family, and community. It's an exciting time!

Most parents are concerned about the talk of "kindergarten readiness." This includes the ability to handle hand washing, regulating behavior while solo and in groups, expressing feelings using words, independently going to the bathroom, and basic skills. Basic skills are things like letter and number identification, writing letters and numbers, writing your name, letter sounds and the beginning or evidence of a growing reader. Reading is a HUGE focus when it comes to kindergarten readiness and it is not uncommon for parents to fear if their child is not reading by the first day of school that they will not be successful. There is a way to lessen the stress and it's simple. Read to your child. The more the child is exposed to reading, the better reader they will become. Read and read consistently. As far as numbers go, expose children to numbers frequently. Point out numbers like addresses, TV channels, clocks, radio stations, recipes, receipts, at the gas station, at stores, menus at restaurants, and while grocery shopping. Get in the habit of helping the child recognize, say, and write numbers to which they are in frequent contact.

Elementary School to Middle School (Junior High)

There are not as many tears for this milestone, yet it is just as important. Like the jump from preschool to elementary, the child is growing in independence and the teachers' expectation for this is increasing. Many elementary schools function with a single class system meaning students are primarily with one teacher that teaches all core subjects for the duration of the day. This is not the case in middle school. In middle school, it is the expectation that students will switch classes multiple times throughout the day as a departmentalized structure is used and teachers now only teach one to two subjects. The additional teachers, with additional personalities, and additional requirements can prove to be a lot for a pre-teen, especially when you factor in those hormonal changes. So middle school calls for a greater need for organization and time management. Organization is what will help the student adjust to the instructor's teaching and communication style, while time management is what will help them stay on top of the work now coming from multiple directions.

While before the anxiety stemmed from the idea of "kindergarten readiness," now the anxiety shifts to what I like to call the 5 Ls: Lockers, Lunch, Location, Laughs, and Learning. Over the years, I have discovered that the #1 concern of most new middle schoolers is…LOCKERS!!! *Lockers* are what the cool kids on all the teen TV shows have, and often the location of all the teen action--- aka "drama." So, naturally it would rank high on the list of all newly entering middle schoolers. They are extremely concerned about not looking like a "loser" if they can't open their locker. The cool factor in middle school is a must as peer pressure is high. Lockers have become such a concern that many schools offer "Locker Days" for the rising middle school students to come before the school year begins to try out the new skill. *Location* deals with the new rooms. Middle schools are bigger than elementary schools and students often fear getting lost and sucked into this imaginary abyss from which they can't escape and if they do, it is only to serve the detention that they'll receive for being late. You know about the detention held in the dungeon like basement of every middle and high school right? For this reason, Open House is a MUST. It gives students a chance to learn the building before the start of the new year. Now for *lunch*. Is the food good or is it the mash potato slop we see in camp movies? Can I sit with my friends or do we have assigned seats? Do I go by myself or with the class in a straight line like a trail of ants? All valid concerns of middle school students and honestly, the answer varies greatly and is dependent on the school's culture.

Laughs, now this can get complex. Laughs equals "laugh with" (friends) and "laugh at" (bullies). We as parents know how important being accepted by your peers is to this age group. It's very much so a self-discovery period. Middle school students often wonder who at school will become their friends and who will become their enemy. You cannot watch a good coming of age movie without the stereotypical bully, so they must exist, right? Keeping the lines of communication open and often informal can help during this time and there are plenty of school personnel and resources to help. Lastly, *learning*: What will we learn this year, and will I be able to keep up? Elementary teachers are known for instilling a little fear in future middle schoolers to get them to act right before leaving. The talk of staying up all night doing homework, and the teacher not spending a lot of time answering questions in class is common scare tactic stuff. So, when it's time to truly make the transition, students may feel unsure if they are equipped to handle this new load. With solid organization strategies and time management skills in place, they will adjust just fine. Another huge adjustment for middle school is actually for the parents, and it comes in the form of communication. The student is getting older and more responsible. Teachers will begin to communicate more directly with the student about their actions regarding academics and behavior. Parents will still remain in the loop, but the step by step or play by play like what was given in elementary school should not be expected.

Middle School to High School

As the road to independence continues, we reach the transition to high school. You should now expect the focus to move from building a student to building an adult. Most actions at this level are preparation for adulthood and post-secondary options be it college or a career. Coming from middle school, students have already adjusted to having multiple classes, learning a large building, lockers, friends and foes, and a greater sense of accountability for their actions. If they were able to get the hang of things, it will make high school much easier because in high school things get intense. In high school, the student becomes the chief decision maker as there is way less parental input. Parents are involved indeed, but their role has changed. In days of the past, parents were the guides and the students followed. As the student gets older, the parent becomes the wise counsel with the student having more authority to make decisions for themselves. These decisions are often not easy, so the anxiety that comes with the transition to high school is rooted in the question, "What do I want to do or be when I grow up?"

A big part of a student's preparation for after high school begins with the selection of classes. Never before have students had so much input in which classes they would like to take. And never before have students had so many options. The selection may include honors, accelerated, advanced placement, early college/dual enrollment, international baccalaureate, vocational education, and various career paths. It is important to note that grade point averages (GPA) become very important in high school as they are used for class rankings and information that may lead to scholarships for postsecondary endeavors. With this being said, it is equally important to note that all classes are not created the same and affect your GPA differently based on possible quality points earned (see Class Types Chapter for the breakdown). In middle school, your GPA and transcript were of a lesser concern, but in high school it becomes a priority.

The amount of self-study demanded at high school is new territory for students too. Teachers expect students to go beyond the classwork given in class for a deeper understanding. They are no longer walking students through the process of learning, but encouraging authentic inquiry. Students that complete work at home and come to class with questions for the teacher often fare better than those that depend on the teacher for discussion. In high school, intrinsic motivation is necessary for success and richer understanding of the material being presented. Surface learning will no longer be enough for mastery at this level.

On a fun note, high school brings countless opportunities to explore passions and gain school spirit as clubs and sports are plentiful, and school activities are endless. The balancing of academic work with extracurricular activities is known to boost a student's confidence, social skills, and support greater achievement in school.

-----Messenger Tips-----

- Attend a transition activity (kindergarten round up, bridging ceremony, Q&A, tours) to learn about the school, expectations at the next level, see the building, and meet the staff. It will help to get some of the nervousness out before the start of the new year.

- Speak to your student about transitioning to the next level and see what concerns they have. Take those questions along with yours to the transition activity and be sure to get the answers to them.

- Be positive about the upcoming milestone. Treat it as an opportunity for a fresh start.

- Expect an adjustment period to occur. This may include grades possibly slipping, organization adjustments, testing parental restrictions and expectations, emotional and behavior ups and downs. The student is simply trying to find their norm in this new environment.

- Take advantage of summer transition prep programs if offered.

- Check your own emotions about the transition and speak to someone that has gone through it before if necessary.

- If the student has special needs, be sure to discuss them with the staff at the new school before the beginning of the new school year.

I WILL HELP MY KID DOMINATE THE SCHOOL YEAR WITHOUT LOSING IT BY...

Educating myself on what is expected at the next school level and using the information to prepare them for this milestone. I know that with each change comes an opportunity for personal and academic growth, and I will encourage them both by supporting the student's studies and progressive independence. I will promote organization, time management, intrinsic motivation, and authentic inquiry to help my child be a forever learner as they build their capacity to later function as a self-sufficient adult.

CHAPTER 4

CLASS TYPES

QUESTION 4: WHAT IS THE DIFFERENCE BETWEEN???

Over the years there has been a steady creation of more diverse classes to meet the needs of our students. The classes range from remediation to standard to advanced. Because of such variety, parents are often confused about the classes, what they offer, how the student is graded, what type of credit is earned, how you qualify for the class, and such. So let's start with the basics. What are some of the different classes now offered in our schools?

Class Types

Traditional/General (Gen Ed): Classes for students performing at grade level. This is your standard class.

Honors: This class is for students performing above grade level. It's usually the same curriculum as that introduced in a traditional class, but it's discussed more in depth. The objectives, or what students are supposed to learn, are more complex. The expected teaching and learning pace is faster than the traditional class.

Accelerated: Very similar to honors, but the curriculum may differ. It is not uncommon for students to receive instruction on both current grade level and next grade level material in this class. The pace is extremely fast as more than a standard year's content is taught.

Advanced Placement (AP): College level courses taught in high school for college credit upon the completion of the course and passing of the accompanied exam. These classes weigh differently for your Grade Point Average or GPA and present the opportunity to earn higher than a 4.0. Example: An "A" in a regular class is worth 4 quality points. An "A" in an AP class is worth 5 quality points thus impacting your GPA more positively. Because these are college level courses, they are more rigorous than a standard high school class. Be aware. Not all colleges will accept AP classes for course credit. If possible, research the colleges of interest and learn which AP classes will count toward college credit BEFORE taking the AP course and test.

Remedial: A service or class for students not performing at grade level. In this environment students are provided with opportunities to master fundamental skills needed to successfully complete work on grade level. Remedial programs are usually offered as pull-out services where the student is pulled from the regular class for additional instruction; extended programming where the student participates in additional instruction before school, after school, or during the summer (summer school); or as a separate class like an "elective." From experience, I've noticed that most remedial programs focus on literacy and mathematics.

Dual Enrollment (DE)/Early College Courses: Courses taken as part of the Dual Enrollment/Early College Program. Classes can be taken online, at the high school, or on the college campus. The program allows high school students to enroll in official college courses while completing high school requirements. Through this program the student starts college "early," or is "dually enrolled" meaning they are now students at two institutions (the high school and college). Through the courses the student may earn credit towards a high school diploma and college degree concurrently. All programs are not the same, so ask questions prior to enrolling. Be aware. Not all colleges will accept dual enrollment credits, so do your research. Especially do your research if your child plans to attend an out of state university. Also, because the courses are actual college classes, the complexity, pacing, and depth of knowledge is higher than that of a standard high school class.

How They Differ?

I'm a visual learner and believe the best way to see the basic differences between the types of classes offered in school is through the use of a table. The "X" means that quality applies for that type of class, or it is "True" for that particular class type. Always double check your school's policy for accuracy. There is no one size fits all to grades and GPA calculations.

(See Table 1.)

	General	Honors	Accelerated	AP	Remedial	DE
Offered at Elementary level	X	X			X	
Offered at Middle Level	X	X	X		X	
Offered at High School level	X	X	X	X	X	X
Graded on unweighted 4.0 GPA Scale at High School Level (standard scale)	X				X	
Graded on weighted 5.0 GPA Scale at High School Level *some districts use a 4.5 scale for Honors		X	X	X		X

Table 1.

Confusion, Chatter, and Cheers!

Because there are now so many different class options, it is easy to get them confused or lost in translation with other programs. So for clarity:

1. Remediation and special education are not the same.
2. Accelerated/Honors does not equal the gifted program.
3. All advanced classes are not college courses.

Remediation vs Special Education

Over the years I have found myself explaining the difference between remedial programs and special education quite frequently. Unfortunately, special education programs have a very negative reputation and most parents want to steer their kids away from them by any means necessary. In my experience, when parents hear that their child is not faring so well in a class and that "remediation" is suggested, 8 out of 10 of them automatically take that as them being placed in special education. It's not. Remediation simply means that we have noticed gaps in the child's learning that we would like to close through the introduction of additional supports. These supports do not qualify the child for the special education program. Key word, *qualify*. You must qualify for special education services, and it can be quite a lengthy process. The

Individuals with Disabilities Education Act (IDEA) is the federal law that defines and regulates special education. According to IDEA, to qualify for special education services a student must:

- Have a documented **disability** that is covered by IDEA, *and*
- Need special education in order to access the general education curriculum

(Lee, n.d., para 8).

Translation:

1. The student has to have a disability listed/covered by IDEA. This disability is not something the teacher or parent has identified themselves, but a trained medical or mental health professional has diagnosed through an evaluation process.

2. The student needs more than a temporary service to learn the general class curriculum successfully. This means that summer school, or before/after school enrichment, or a remedial elective class alone will not close the identified gaps or provide enough support for continuous academic growth of the student. This also suggests that the disability interferes with the

learning of the grade-level material. Additional resources and modifications are needed for the child to be able to learn or master the material at the desired level. Whether the student does "need special education" is determined through the districts' evaluation process.

School districts all have a special education qualifying process in place that involves a comprehensive evaluation. The comprehensive evaluation will examine the child's development in multiple areas as well as a look into how the child processes information. A simple recommendation for additional academic support does not equal admittance into the special education program.

Accelerated/Honors vs The Gifted Program (Gifted Student)

No doubt that a student has to have a heightened intelligence level and capacity for learning to take accelerated and honors classes, but that ability alone does not qualify them as a gifted learner. Key word again, *qualify*. Strong class averages and standardized test scores are usually needed to gain access to honors and accelerated classes, but they are not the only criteria for the gifted and talented student classification. The federal government defines "Gifted & Talented" students as:

The term "gifted and talented", when used with respect to students, children, or youth, means students, children, or youth who give evidence of high achievement capability in areas such as intellectual, creative, artistic, or leadership capacity, or in specific academic fields, and who need services or activities not ordinarily provided by the school in order to fully develop those capabilities ("20 U.S.Code. Section 7801," 2018).

Translation:

Students considered gifted have not only the ability, but a proven record of excellence in the area of their giftedness be it intellect, creative, leadership, the arts, etc. They are abstract thinkers and creative problem solvers that require access to resources beyond what is offered to the traditional student to fully develop their talents.

Students must go through an extensive evaluation process to be determined gifted and talented. However, "There are no nationwide or even statewide standards for identification. Each school district makes a determination about which and how many students it is able to service within its programs based on its definitions, philosophy and resources" ("Giftedness Defined-NSGT," 2018).

So, there is definitely a difference between a smart kid, and a gifted student as determined by the school system.

Therefore, you can have gifted students in honors classes, but that doesn't make *all* honor class students gifted.

Advanced Classes vs College Credit Courses

There are many high school offerings of advance level classes, but they do not all yield college credit. Traditionally classes like AP, Dual-enrollment, and sometimes International Baccalaureate (IB) courses offer an opportunity to earn college credit. We want to make sure not to confuse quality points and the weighted GPA scale with college credit. A class may very well earn a student additional quality points that lead to a GPA over 4.0, but that does not mean that that particular class earned the student college credit. You can earn additional quality points without earning college credit. When in doubt, head to the student handbook or the grade level counselor. Both can provide a breakdown for how it works at your child's school.

-----Messenger Tips-----

- Know your child's strengths and weaknesses. This will be beneficial when selecting courses.
- Ask for an evaluation. If you believe your child may benefit from services given through special education, be it self-contained instruction, or the gifted and tal-

ented program, ask the teacher/counselor about the evaluation process. Also keep in mind that special education does not only address intellectual and learning disabilities, but also behavioral, emotional, and other impairments.

- Consider your child's academic goals, extracurricular, and family commitments before deciding on participation in courses. We want to support the best learning environment for our children that offers opportunities for growth. What we don't want to do is completely stress them out by taking on more than they are able to do successfully. I've seen families encourage students to take a full load of advance classes and the students blossom with their support. I've also had parents in my office crying because their kids don't go to bed until after 2am every night, and they have had to cancel all family outings and extracurricular activities during the school year because of the child's workload. Both the student and parent were completely burnt out and at the point of despair.

- Remember that the older the child gets, the more of a guide and reference you become. Parents will not be responsible for completing the work of the class-- the student will. Because of this, it is important that we remember to allow our children to be the decision maker when choosing classes (we can make suggestions).

**I WILL HELP MY KID DOMINATE THE SCHOOL YEAR
WITHOUT LOSING IT BY...**

Knowing about the various class options available at the
school and discussing with them which are best for their
learning. I will empower my child to consider the pros and
cons of the offerings thus making them invested in the process and accountable for the decision and the responsibilities
that come with it.

CHAPTER 5

GRADES

QUESTION 5: HOW ARE THEY CALCULATED AND WHAT DO THEY MEAN?

If I had a dime for every time a parent asked me, "why didn't my child's grade go up?" I would be crazy rich! And usually they would ask this after one good test grade or completed homework assignment. Let me help US. First things first, ALL ASSIGNMENTS ARE NOT CREATED EQUAL. Not hardly. Most don't know this, so this is where the majority of the confusion stems. I'm a visual learner, so I want to supply a visual for this lesson. Once a teacher, always a teacher. In the image below there are four coins, and we have one of each coin. Though we have the same quantity of each coin (1), their *values* are not the same. One quarter is worth 25 cents while one dime is worth only 10 cents.

Grades for assignments work the same way. Students receive assignments in multiple categories and each category has a designated percentage *weight (value)*. Common categories are homework, classwork, projects, and assessments/tests. Using those categories let's take a look at this table.

Category	Weight
Homework	10%
Classwork	30%
Projects	20%
Assessments	40%
Total	100%

As you can see, homework assignments are not worth as much as classwork just like a dime is not worth as much as a quarter. This concept factors heavily into the student's grade. It takes three times as many homework assignments to equal one classwork assignment. Therefore, it will take three 100% homework assignments to equal one 100% classwork assignment. So, if you are wondering why Johnny's 98 on last night's Math homework improved his grade by just 1% while the 40 on the math test dropped his grade by 10%, this is why (and those figures are purely for example).

It is important for students and parents to understand how grades are calculated so that they can effectively monitor progress. If a student is struggling in a class, one of the quickest ways to improve their grade would be to improve the area with the highest weighted percentage. In this example, a "90" on a test would have a greater impact on the final grade than a "90" on a homework assignment. There are other factors that may affect the calculation of grades, like the amount of assignments in each category, but this is enough information for now to get us headed in the right direction.

The breakdown of categories and weights is usually found on the class syllabus. If there is a schoolwide or districtwide grade weight policy that information is normally in the student handbook. And as always, you can look online at "gradebook/parent portal/online campus" to see the categories and percentages too. *Gradebook* is the generic name for the online tool that parents use to monitor grades, attendance, and sometimes behavior as well.

Alphabet Soup

Grade percentages are the numerical representation of how a student fares in class, but there is also a letter grade associated with the values. The common A, B, C, D, F system is used mostly starting around grade 3 with an E, S, U, N/NI system used for primary levels. I've taught at schools where a 70 was a "D" and others where it was a "C." There are districts where a failing grade was anything below a 70 and others failing was below a 60. What constitutes a letter grade will vary depending on the school's grading scale so make sure to check the school's handbook, class syllabus, or school website for that info. Also keep in mind that some districts have gotten rid of the "D" altogether to create what can be translated as "either you know it or you don't" system.

Grade	Meaning	
A	Excelling/Excellent	
B	Good	
C	Fair/Average	
D	Below Average	
F	Failing	
Grade	Meaning	Think
E	Excellent	A
S	Satisfactory	B/C
U	Unsatisfactory	D
N/NI	Needs Improvement	F

Since we are discussing grades, let me share this truth. Not all completed work is graded work. There I said it. Sorry teachers. Some work is very informal and though reviewed does not make it to the gradebook. If you are wondering what happened to that assignment you worked on with little Johnny, this might be the answer. Now don't fret. Teachers have to make sure that they give ample opportunity to master a skill before grading work. When your child tells you that they aren't sure what they made on that assignment, in some cases that may be true. When in doubt ask the teacher, and if your student is middle school and above, have *them* ask their teacher. We have to teach our kids to speak up for (advocate) themselves as early as possible.

Grades vs GPA

I would love to say there's an ultra-easy way to describe this, but I haven't found one. So, here's *The Messenger's Way:*

Grades- Values given for a single assignment/assessment that leads to a class average.

Grade Point Average (GPA)- The numerical representation of the average of all class grades as calculated using a 4 or 5 point scale.

Technical Definition for GPA:

A *grade point average* is a number representing the average value of the accumulated final grades earned in courses over time. More commonly called a *GPA*, a student's grade point average is calculated by adding up all accumulated final grades and dividing that figure by the number of grades awarded. This calculation results in a mathematical mean— or average—of all final grades (The Glossary of Education Reform, 2013).

One of the most noticeable changes regarding class grades and GPA is the different scale used. A GPA is normally calculated using a 4 point scale in which an "A" class average is worth 4 pts, a "B" is worth 3 points, a "C" is worth 2 points, a "D" is worth 1 point, and a failing grade earns 0 points. The averaging of all courses taken within a specific time frame is the GPA. Keep in mind that GPA is a conversation of relevance often introduced at the high school level as a ranking system for post-secondary education options (college and such). Sometimes you'll hear about GPA in middle school, but that's not typical.

STOP! How many of us have heard parents on social media proudly announcing their child's 4.33 GPA and thought, how is that even possible? Well it is. It is possible to earn higher than a 4.0 if the high school recognizes a *weighted scale* (5.0). I know this is a lot, but stay with me. A weighted scale is when the difficulty of the class is considered as part of the GPA calculations. This comes into play when students take advanced level classes like advanced placement (AP) courses which are college level classes. Well the rigor of those courses is what qualifies them for "extra points." Think of it this way. The effort it takes to make a "B" in a college level class while in high school is most likely equivalent to the effort it takes to make an "A" in a standard high school class ;therefore, they both receive the same amount of points...4. When calculating a GPA using a weighted scale, an "A" is worth 5pts, a "B" is worth 4pts, a "C" is worth 3pts, and we'll stop there. If your child is in an advanced level course, Ds and Fs really shouldn't be an option. If he/she, is making that low of a grade, you may need to reconsider this option. Even a "C" is frowned upon in an advanced level course and signals that a quick recovery or another class option may be necessary. More discussion on this when we address the various class types offered in school.

Transcripts

The grade conversation can be a bit much, but transcripts are actually pretty straight forward. Transcripts are the complete record of your child's academic performance while in school. Transcripts can show an all-inclusive academic history or just the records for that particular school level. If your child is in the fifth grade, the transcript will cover grades K-5. If they are a senior in high school, the transcript will cover grades 9-12. No need for their 1st grade assessment scores by this point. Transcripts are necessary when seeking post high school graduation options and should be reviewed periodically for accuracy. Transcripts/school records may also be requested when enrolling in school. This gives the new institution a chance to get a first look at performance levels and possible needed supports.

-------Messenger Tips-------

- Review the class syllabus or student handbook *with* the student at the beginning of each new school year for each class. The breakdown of weights for categories may not be the same for all classes.

- Check grades online at the beginning of the quarter to get an idea how the weights work without the clutter of tons of assignments in the system.

- Ask for help! If you cannot figure out how grades are calculated in gradebook, log in to the system and ask the teacher to walk you through the process. Ask not, know not.

- If you are a visual learner YouTube saves lives and hours of headaches. Simply search for a video on how grades and GPA are calculated. I'm not offended at all. It's called "reinforcement."

- Come up with a system for staying current on your child's academic progress and follow through. DO NOT become the parent that waits until the end of the grading period to start asking questions about how things are done and how did your child earn a particular grade (more discussion about this later).

I WILL HELP MY KID DOMINATE THE SCHOOL YEAR WITHOUT LOSING IT BY...

Reviewing the class syllabus or student handbook early in the year with my child so that we both understand how grades are calculated and what those values mean when it comes to academic achievement or skill mastery. Knowing this information will help me as a parent understand my child's progression in a class and will help my child to be more accountable for their learning.

CHAPTER 6

HOMEWORK

QUESTION 6: HOW DO I HELP WITH HOMEWORK WITHOUT GOING CRAZY?

And then there's...HOMEWORK. We love it, we hate it. It's a double edged sword. We understand the importance of it, its value, but could do without the tension it often brings to our homes. One thing we teachers know about homework and parents is that it can be overwhelming. There is a hidden belief that most parents have that we need to dismantle immediately! What is it? What's the belief? The idea that parents must morph into certified classroom teachers to assist their children with homework is so widespread and false that it's the first area I want to tackle. Say it with me, "The home is an extension of the classroom, but not the classroom." Now we are all well aware that parents are intelligent, versatile, creative, and highly skilled in a multitude of areas, but they are not responsible for the standards-based instruction initiated by the classroom teacher. When it comes to homework, it is most important that parents are a triple threat: supportive, resourceful, and aware. That's our role. That's our lane. That's where we exist. Now let's dive deeper.

Role 1: Supportive

When we become parents, we automatically enroll in the school of motivational speaking. From day one, we mumble words of encouragement to those little bundles of joy we call our children. We encourage them to speak, to roll, to eat, to crawl, to walk, and so much more. As they get older, we encourage them to trust their instincts and take risks. This same level of positive encouragement is needed during homework time. We have to remind our children of their strengths and abilities and how practicing makes what's once presumed hard, easy. The purpose of homework is to practice a skill for eventual mastery. That's it! Homework is an opportunity to practice or reinforce a skill, not a means of torture. So often our kids have a negative perception of homework because WE have a negative *reaction* to homework. We'll say things like, "You have to do all of this? Get started so you can get it over with. Do it so you can be done and go outside and play." Listen to the tone of those words! "Do it so you can be done and go outside and play." Clearly "play" is the priority here and the homework is simply the obstacle in the way of the priority. Now you may not have used these exact words, but how many of us have said things similar? Exactly. Well, how do we think kids will begin to feel (if not already resenting it) about homework after we react to it in this manner? So being supportive means keep a positive stance about homework and speak to the benefits of it more than the drawbacks.

What motivates your child? What gives them a boost of energy? Be aware of what works to re-energize your child after a slump. The motivator may be something tangible or not. Teach them how to set goals big and small. Intrinsic motivation will be more beneficial to you as an adult than any toy or candy could ever be. Intrinsic motivation is our drive to excel, and it is developed from setting goals and working to accomplish them. This self-motivation is what is needed to successfully finish not just homework, but life. As a support system we are there to help when needed, and not to take over. If our children come to us with questions about the work, it is okay to assist them in finding the answers. Plus, we need to applaud them for taking the initiative to ask for help. That's huge! Homework is ultimately our kid's responsibility and should never become *our* work. We don't have homework, they do. Let the responsibility fall where it should and give every opportunity for our maturing youngster to step up to the plate to handle it. Will we be more hands on in the early years (K-2)? Of course. But as our children get older, our desire to assist or review every problem should diminish. No fear. There is still a way for us to stay on top of what should be or needs to be done and how our angels are progressing. Which brings us to our second role.

Role 2: Aware

As parents, we should be aware of what homework our children have. This awareness may not come in the form of a moment by moment update, but it does require us having a general notion of what should be done. How we get this information is going to depend on the grade level of the student. It is much easier to keep up with assignments for elementary and middle school students than high schoolers. Why? In elementary school, there is ample communication with parents about work in the form of weekly newsletters, weekly folders, or maybe even a weekly email. At that level, we are more hands on and teachers are pretty good about giving us the heads up on what students are learning in class and at home. Many teachers will go as far as listing the weekly homework on their website or in the newsletters. A quick glance at either and you are usually caught up to speed on what your child should work on for the week. Now right around fourth grade things will begin to change. Teachers are placing more responsibility on the student and may require them to write assignments in an agenda book or check the website themselves. Middle school is very similar. By this point, students are no longer bringing home weekly folders or newsletters for the parents to view. This means that more dialogue with the student is needed to see what is on the homework agenda. However, technology is big in middle school, and it is not uncommon for teachers to post the work on their websites. Remember, we are not promoting helicopter parenting strategies. I refuse to tell you to stand over a child to repeatedly ask them "What do you have for homework?" I am simply stressing how to stay in the loop and periodic checks are good enough. Again, homework is the child's responsibility, but it is our duty to be aware of what our student is responsible for and how they are progressing. In order to be aware, you have to know where to look and who to ask. The *who* to ask is simple, your child. Always start there, especially if the student is in the third grade or higher. If you find yourself constantly asking about homework and the child is hesitant to answer or doesn't have an answer, it's time to investigate. Jump on the school's online parent portal system to check grades to see how the child is progressing. Grades are a telltale of if the work is being done and if it is being done correctly. This is especially important in high school as there are fewer ways for parents to know what work the student is responsible for doing. The older the child, the more direct communication the teachers are having with them. It's all in preparation for adulthood. When you are an adult, information is no longer being filtered down through your parents. We have to start somewhere.

Being aware is more complex than just knowing what worksheet has to be done, or what project needs to be completed. Being aware also involves knowing what skills are being covered. What is the child actually learning? When we know what the student is learning and not just the product they are responsible for creating, we can really be beneficial to the team. Which brings us to our third role.

Role 3: Resourceful

If I know what you are learning, I can help you master it by finding resources for you. Gone are the days of feeling like we are back in school struggling to figure out a problem. In walks technology and the internet. Parents no longer have to feel like we know all the answers to our kids' work. We just have to know where to look to find the answers. I don't have to know how to speak French to help my child with his French homework. The internet is very useful when it comes to this. A quick Google search and a plethora of options pop up in seconds to serve as an aid. Now the real work may come in the form of vetting the sources. My solution is to try multiple sites to see if the information is similar. I also compare what I know against what is presented on the site. Speaking of websites, don't forget the teacher's website. It is common practice for teachers to link their most used resources to their teacher page. This is a plus because the sites are often used in class and therefore the student is familiar with how to navigate it. I know of teachers that would list the weekly homework on their website and supply a link to show you how to do the work right next to each problem. How crazy is that? What other help could you need if they take those additional steps? Sometimes it's just about knowing what resources are available at your disposal. Who are we kidding, it's *all* about knowing which resources are available to use. No reinventing the wheel here. If the school supplies the resources, use them. This requires you visiting the school website and the teacher pages so that you have an idea of what information is available to you long before you actually need it. Also, speak to your child. Ask them where they can look for extra help. Ask them what resources they use in class for this type of work. Remember, homework should be an extension of what was introduced prior in class. Unless your child is in a *flipped classroom* environment, what is presented as homework should not be a new concept, but review.

Is old school more your speed? Not a problem. Books, board games, manipulatives, siblings, study groups, and tutors still work and are all viable options. There is actually a movement amongst affluent families all over the country (including Silicon Valley-the irony) to discontinue the use of technology/screen-time in school and go back to simpler methods (Bowles, 2018). The concern is that our children are becoming so dependent on technology that they are losing most of their soft skills like solid communication techniques. If you have this concern or are simply just looking for variety, don't forget to use some of the other aforementioned options that may be technology free. I personally am a fan of manipulatives, flash cards, and study groups. The maneuvering of objects with manipulatives incorporates multiple senses that may better connect the student's learning style to the learning task. Flash cards offer a chance to master vocabulary, equations, or facts through the self-quiz or partner quiz model. Study groups give students the opportunity to discuss in detail the material and hear different perspectives on problem solving from peers. Sometimes peers serve as the best teachers as they may be more relatable with more relevant explanations to a similar aged audience. No offense older people. As we can see, we have options outside of the internet that we are more than free to use. They were effective before, and contrary to this "new kids new learning" theory, they are still effective now. There, I said it.

Other resources to use are the school's parent workshops and resource centers. Make sure to check school announcements for upcoming workshop dates and plan to attend the ones that meet your most pressing needs. Workshops for reading and that dreaded *math* are pretty popular, so be on the lookout for those. As far as parent resource centers, not all schools have them so be sure to ask if your school has one. If you are lucky enough to have one, take advantage of it. You can check out books, games, and other supplies to use at home with the student. One cool thing about parent resource centers is that they usually have someone running it. Ding ding ding! That person is a resource too! Be sure to ask them questions on additional best strategies to help your child with their work.

As we can see, there are ways we can help our kids with homework without going crazy. You may have noticed, I have yet to recommend one single content related strategy to help our kids with homework. This was not by mistake. I intentionally wanted you to see how we can be effective without having to be masters of the content or the class teacher. As our kids get older, the work will get harder and there will be things we don't remember or know. I wanted to break the habit of thinking that we have to have all the answers. We simply must know where to look and the importance of promoting values such as responsibility/accountability, self-motivation, and pride in your work. Becoming familiar with specific strategies to promote subject area mastery is extra and the icing on the cake.

------- Messenger Tips-------

- YouTube is our friend. Use it to search for videos on your chosen topic. You will find that many teachers record their lessons and place them on that platform for student use. Now we can use them too.

- Have a central area for homework and make sure that it is stocked with supplies like paper, pens, pencils, color pencils, markers, post-its, highlighters, a dictionary and thesaurus, etc. Also have technology available if needed for student work.

- Make a cheat sheet of useful websites by subject and post it close to the homework area. Also create a folder online under "favorites" and save all the links there.

- Create a homework schedule and stick to it. When will the student begin homework? What is the cutoff time? Will they have a snack? Be allowed to play outside before or after homework? Make sure to account for any extracurricular activities on the schedule.

- Ask questions about the learning. Ask your child to explain what they are learning. Show you how to do a problem. Read the homework directions or a couple questions to you. This interaction between you and them communicates your interest and investment in what they are doing.

- Look for opportunities to expand the learning. Point out connections to what they are learning to what you experience in real life. Use everyday activities or field trips to do this.

- Teach your child to advocate for themselves. Make sure they know the importance of asking for help and how to do it. They can ask you for help, a peer, the teacher, or another adult. Role play if necessary.

- You ask the teacher for help (for younger students). They have a wealth of knowledge on exactly what your student needs.

I WILL HELP MY KID DOMINATE THE SCHOOL YEAR WITHOUT LOSING IT BY...

Being a triple threat when it comes to homework. I will be supportive, aware, and resourceful. I will not place stress on myself to become the "teacher." I will make sure to keep a positive attitude and outlook when assisting with homework. Overwhelm often is a product of last minute demands therefore I will use a variety of means to stay aware of what my child is learning, assignments, and resources to support them. I will also make sure that the responsibility of the work remains with my child along with the rewards and consequences of their efforts.

CHAPTER 7

Parent-Teacher Conferences

QUESTION 7: WHAT SHOULD I EXPECT AND HOW DO I PRE-PARE?

It's not officially a school year until the parent-teacher conferences are held. They are staples in our school programs.

Over the years they have taken on many looks like teacher led, student led, parent led, or even small group. One thing has remained the same, the goal. The goal of any conference is *strategy*. Yes, you are being informed of the student's progress. Yes, you may even be shown samples of work. But do keep in mind the core focus of *how do we move the student forward?*

Conference Expectations

The discussion will be on the academic, social, and behavioral progress of the student, attendance (if need be), and the completion of time sensitive paperwork. You will hear about the student's strengths and how to nurture them, along with any areas of concern. Areas of concern are usually where the majority of the time is spent as you must all work together to strategize and create an action plan to fix it. Please know that the accountability factor will be high as all parties (teacher, parent/family, student) will be expected to work together consistently to rectify the issue. Conferences are wonderful times to share student portfolios or work samples so there is a visual of the student's performance and level of mastery. So, do expect to see work and ask for samples or examples if it is not readily available. At this meeting, also expect to update your contact information and discuss the best way to monitor academic and behavioral progress at school.

Conference Preparation

My #1 tip for parents who plan to attend conferences is to…plan ahead. I have witnessed too many times parents coming in with tons of questions and leaving with zero answers. They were simply all over the place with thoughts and emotions and the conference was more of a gripe session than a work session. Conferences should be productive, and you must be strategic. There will be a limited amount of time so it is important to maximize each minute. The best way to do this is to come with questions, observations, and concerns written down. Begin with a general list. Jot down whatever comes to mind when thinking about your child's progress in school/class. Once you make the list, review it and prioritize it. Try to narrow your questions, comments/concerns, and observations to 5 things then star the top three. Your top three make up the "I must have answered before I leave" list. Why three? The teacher will have items to discuss as well. We want the conference to have more of a conversational feel than an interrogation vibe. PLUS...we want to listen. We NEED to listen. We have to intentionally listen to what is being said at the conference from all involved parties so we know how best to support the unified mission of progress. If you find that you have way more than 5 items to discuss, that is a sign that more frequent communication is needed. We should not have a grocery list of discussion topics at a conference. Consistent communication with both the teacher and the student should eliminate the extensive list. I say this out of love. Do not allow the mass accumulation of questions, comments, and concerns to build in hopes that they will all be answered or resolved at a conference. There's simply not enough time for all of that. Get in the habit of communicating regularly about progress and such with the teacher. If your child is in secondary school (middle or high school), make it a point of frequently communicating about academic progress with them as well. They are now at the age where they can begin to advocate for themselves and articulate the happenings. The conference should not be full of grand reveals as you have a system of staying in the loop in place. Once the conference is over, review what was discussed with the student to make sure everyone is on the same page and aware of the expectations and next steps. If the student is doing well, celebrate them and let them know how proud you are and to keep going. If the student is not doing well, motivate them and remind them that together things will get better and to keep going.

Teacher Jargon Glossary

Sometimes it seems like teachers have a language of their own. They often speak in acronyms and buzzwords unfamiliar to many not in education. Here's a quick translation of 21 common terms and phrases often used in parent-teacher conferences.

1. *Accommodations-* a change to or in your child's learning <u>environment</u> NOT the content they are expected to learn. Environment may mean the class or factors relating to time/length of time for tasks.

2. *AP-(Advanced Placement)* College-level courses taught in high school for college credit upon the completion of the course and passing of the accompanied exam. These classes weigh differently for your GPA and may affect them positively. Example: An "A" in a regular education class is worth 4 GPA points. An "A" in an AP class is worth 5 GPA points.

3. *Assessments*-Form of evaluation of work. Most commonly referencing "TESTS." Assessments may include class, district level, state level, and national level *testing*.

4. *Curriculum*-A detailed outline of what's being taught in class...PERIOD

5. *Gifted*-(Gifted and Talented/ Talented and Gifted) a program for students deemed to function with a high level of intellectual and creative abilities and able to achieve academically at an accelerated pace. It is part of the Special Education Program and students must be tested into it.

6. *GPA-(Grade Point Average)* An indication of a student's academic achievement and the cumulative average of all grades for a specified period of time. Most common scale is the 4.0 scale. A= 4, B=3pts, C=2pts, D=1pt, F=0pts.

7. *Grading Scale*-The range for each letter grade. Ex: A=90-100, B=80-89, etc. The scale varies by schools/districts so be sure to ask about it.

8. *Grading Weights*- The percentage a task (classwork, homework, projects, assessments, etc.) weighs. ALL TASKS ARE NOT CREATED EQUAL. Usually, assessments count way more

than classwork, quizzes, and definitely home-work. Ask for the breakdown to stay on top of it. This is why the homework your child made an "A" on didn't change his overall grade.

9. *IEP- (Individual Education Plan)* every student receiving special education services has to have an IEP. The IEP must include the services, supports, accommodations, and modifications the school will provide to help the student progress and meet their annual goals. IEPs are legally binding documents and everything outlined in it must be carried out. The document is updated at least an-nually.

10. *Lexile Scores*-Scores represent a student's reading level on a developmental scale. The score shows what range of material the student should be able to comprehend comfortably. Lexile scores *are not the same* as grade levels. You will, however, see Lexile scores and grade equivalents on standard-ized testing for student performance comparison reasons.

11. *Make-up Policy-* How long a student has to com-plete and return work missed from an absence without penalty. This can get tricky! Stay on top of it.

12. *Modifications*-a change in what a student is expected to learn and demonstrate. Example. The class is learning about 5 historical figures and must do a report on each. A student with a modification may only learn about 3 and have to report on those. The workload and product have been "modified."

13. *Performance Tasks*-Usually a more hands-on engaging way for students to show mastery of a skill (more so than traditional pen and paper responses). A chance for students to creatively interpret what they've learned.

14. *Proficient*-Child is working at grade level in this area or they have mastered the skill. Good Work!

15. *Progressing*- A teacher's nice way of saying "the child is not performing on grade level. They are behind and working to catch up."

16. *Promotion Criteria*- What the student needs to take and pass to move on to the next grade level.

17. *Remediation*-Extra assistance offered to help the student perform at grade level. THIS DOES NOT EQUAL SPECIAL EDUCATION. Remediation is extra academic support. Special Ed-

ucation is a completely different education program that the student is tested into.

18. *Rigor*-An educator's favorite "buzzword." It simply means more complex and thought provoking work. We don't want the kids to just know the "who, what, and where," but also the "how and why."

19. *School-Parent Compact*- The outlined plan that explains how parents, students, and the school will achieve positive results in a chosen target area like literacy or math. These plans are mandatory for all Title I schools AND all parent have to sign a paper saying that they received a copy of it.

20. *Standards*- learning goals for what students should know and be able to do at each grade level. Yes, the very unpopular *Common Core* is a state standards initiative. Many districts have their own standards that are a version of *Common Core*.

21. *Title I*- a federally supported program that offers funding to schools with a high population of students in poverty as determined by percentage of students receiving free and/or reduced lunch. All funding MUST be used for resources to support

student academic achievement. Basically, it provides money for resources to close the achievement gap between the have and have nots .

-----Messenger Tips-----

- PREPARE IN ADVANCE. Have your questions, comments, and concerns written down before arriving.

- Make sure to get your "top 3" answered before leaving.

- Listen to all parties in attendance at the conference. They all play a role in your child's success.

- Be excited about your child's progress and encouraging about their needs. Energy is contagious and positive is more helpful than negative.

- Need help thinking of questions to ask at the conference? A quick web search will deliver plenty. Try asking, "Is my child performing on grade-level? In what areas are they excelling? In what areas do they need extra help? What resources can I use at home to support their learning? May I share information with you about a situation at home? How is my child adjusting socially and emotionally? Is there anything we can start working on now that will help my child with the work that's coming in the future? Can you explain what this score/grade/evaluation means? Do you have any questions for me?"

- Most conferences have academic and behavioral focuses, but if you have questions or concerns dealing with social and emotional development, feel free to express those too. Also, if there is something going on at home that may affect the child's learning at school do share that information as well.

I WILL HELP MY KID DOMINATE THE SCHOOL YEAR WITHOUT LOSING IT BY...

Preparing my questions, comments, and concerns for the conference in advance so that we may maximize the time spent. I will also hold all parties, including myself and my child, accountable for following through with the necessary steps to show or continue progress in all areas discussed (academic, behavioral, attendance, social, and etc.). Being proactive and consistent is the best way to eliminate unnecessary stress and my child and I will continue to strive to be both.

CHAPTER 8

Title I

QUESTION 8: DOES THIS MEAN THE SCHOOL IS FAILING?

All of my teaching experience was gained from a Title I school. Every ounce of it. It's the world that I know best. Interestingly enough, I never viewed my students as misfortunate, disadvantaged, or impoverished like the federal guidelines, statistics, and stereotypes would tell you. I simply saw my kids as...students. They were students of various backgrounds including religion, race, class, aptitude, life experiences, motivations, and so much more. It never failed that they were an interesting bunch, a tossed salad of personalities. So imagine the disgust that I felt when the Title I conversations erupted. How shocked I was to discover others' perception of students like mine without any formal introduction. For those only familiar with Title I through the grapevine, the assumptions are plentiful. Allow me to shed light on the situation. Because the best way to explain Title I is to discuss the many myths surrounding it. And we aren't short of those.

First things first, what is Title I?

According to the US Department of Education, Title I is the oldest and largest federally funded program originally enacted in the 1965 Elementary and Secondary Education Act (ESEA) as a way to provide funds to schools to close the achievement gap between low-income students and their higher income peers (US Department of Education, 2018 & Clark, 2018). When No Child Left Behind (NCLB) was introduced in 2001 it added an extra layer of accountability for the schools. Schools now had to show adequate yearly progress on state testing in order to continue receiving Title I funding. NCLB has since been replaced by the 2015 Every Student Succeeds Act (ESSA) that describes the purpose of Title I as:

SEC. 1001. STATEMENT OF PURPOSE.

The purpose of this title is to provide all children significant opportunity to receive a fair, equitable, and high-quality education, and to close educational achievement gaps (ESSA 2015).

As we can see, the goal of the program has not changed that much through the years.

Now a look at the myths surrounding the Title I Program.

Myth 1: Title I schools are ALL failing schools.

False: Simply put, Title I funding is in place to level the playing field between the have and have nots by providing supplemental resources to promote academic achievement. As a result, there are Title I schools that are considered high achieving, competitive, and even outperforming Non-Title I schools. Are there also Title I schools not meeting standards? Yes, there are and quite a few. There is an undeniable correlation between poverty and academic achievement. However, ALL Title I schools are not failing schools therefore the Title I descriptor alone does not guarantee the education will be subpar. It is not an automatic indicator that the school is not meeting state standards or *failing*.

Myth 2: Title I resources are only for poor kids.

False: While a school does have to have a high percentage of *disadvantaged* students to **qualify** for Title I funding (40% population or higher for schoolwide programs and lower percentages for targeted programs), the lower income students are not the only ones receiving Title I resources and services (NCES Fast Facts, 2018). If a school is designated Title I "targeted," students considered to be at greatest risk academically will receive resources regardless of socioeconomic status. Translation, "they don't have to be poor to receive services." Schools designated as having a Title I "schoolwide program," afford Title I resources to ALL the students attending the school regardless of income level. Students identified as most at risk for not meeting state academic standards receive *additional* resources under this model. I have personally worked at a Title I school that had million dollar homes and children of celebrities in its attendance area. Were those kids poor? No. Did they benefit from the school's Title I resources and services (new technology, smaller class sizes, additional instructional support)? Absolutely.

Myth 3: Title I schools are for minority students.

False: Title I schools are determined by the income-level of students and not the race. The demographics of a school are determined by the location of the school and those who populate the area. However, it's no secret that minority families on average have lower family incomes than their white counterparts and therefore are disproportionately represented in Title I Schools (pewsocialtrends.org, 2016).

Myth 4: Title I schools get millions of dollars.

False: The amount of money a school gets for Title I assistance is determined by the population of the school and those qualifying as "disadvantaged." There is not a standard amount that every Title I school gets.

Myth 5: Schools can spend their funds on whatever they like. (The Blank Check Myth)

False: In the world of Title I, every dollar must be spent to promote academic achievement of the student in some form or fashion. That is the purpose of the program. The idea that school staff is somehow living lavishly on Title I funds is a bit of a stretch. Title I budgets have to be drafted and approved, then approved again before a single cent can be spent. The majority of most Title I budgets are spent on staffing teachers as support specialist or to reduce class size. Technology and afterschool/weekend/summer academic enrichment programs, or Pre-K programs are also popular Title I budget items.

Myth 6: Schools are allowed to run their Title I program however they choose. There are no checks and balances in place.

False: Title I schools have mandatory annual requirements to meet that are monitored at the district level, the state level, and beyond. One of those requirements is the annual Title I Planning Meeting. All things Title I are discussed at this meeting including how the school is performing academically (including test results), goals for the upcoming school year, how the budget was spent this year, how the budget should be spent next year, how the school plans to keep families in the loop, and more. The meeting is open to all stakeholders. Stakeholders are members of the school community including staff, parents, students, and community businesses and leaders. The purpose of the meeting is to *get input* on how to move the school forward based on the current information (data). Schools are not supposed to hold these meetings without the review and suggestions of parents and the community. If you ever wanted to know how all that Title I money is spent or how the school is faring compared to others, this is the meeting for you. This meeting is usually held at the beginning of the school year or at the conclusion of the year before summer break. Note, this is just one of many Title I activities that happen during the school year; however, in my opinion, it's the best one to get you caught up on the basics of a Title I program.

Myth 7: Title I schools bring down property values.

Inconclusive: This myth does not directly affect student academic performance, but is definitely a big part of the Title I conversation. However, while it's a known truth that affluent communities usually have high performing schools and vice versa, the research available on this topic contained way too many variables to consider to make a direct connection to the Title I program. In the research I viewed, it was hard to determine if schools were the driving force that impacted the property values in the community or if the property values of the community was the force that impacted the schools. Affluence is associated with property values with higher priced homes being connected to more financially stable and educated families and lower income homes are associated with the reverse point of view. With that being said and considering the financial hardship criteria associated with the Title I program, we can assume that average property values would be lower in Title I zoned areas than those that are not.

Myth 8: Title I programs destroy schools

No…and Yes: SHOCKER! Here's what I've noticed. Are you ready for this unfiltered truth? The program itself does not destroy the school, but how the community reacts to it does. There is such a negative connotation associated with Title I that the mere mention of it in some communities causes residents to put homes up for sale in fear of the quick demise of the school. The Title I stamp on a school is supposed to signify that the school will now receive additional funding to provide for supplemental resources to enhance the academic experience of the students and aid in them meeting state academic standards. Instead many read it as the invasion of the poverty stricken, uncouth, unmotivated, intellectually challenged, and usually minority students and their non-participatory parents. These stereotypes associated with the program are, in my opinion, what causes the once invested staff and families to cut ties in an attempt to disassociate and save themselves from the impending doom of the school.

This constant exiting of staff and families causes a revolving door effect which makes it hard to reestablish a progressive academic program and usually leads to a drop in the school's academic performance. Now I could go on and on about THIS, but that's a separate book...

-----Messenger Tips-----

- Don't believe the rumor mill. If you really want to know about Title I, go to a meeting. Ask questions. This info is not top secret and schools are required to post their Title I annual updates and have access to documents at all time for community review.

- Find out who's the administrator over the school's Title I program or who's the family engagement representative. They will have the information you need or can lead you in the right direction.

- If you know of resources or programs that can help support academic growth of students, make sure to give that information to the school Title I administrators or representatives early in the year for consideration. You can only use funding for programs and resources that are documented and budget approved.

- You beat fear with knowledge. The more we know about a subject the less speculation we have.

I WILL HELP MY KID DOMINATE THE SCHOOL YEAR WITHOUT LOSING IT BY...

Learning as much as I can about the Title I Program (if it applies to my child's school) including contacts, requirements, and resources and dismissing the rumor mill. I will also advocate for the best usage of funds to support student learning and ask questions when needed. I know that with proper channels in place my child has a greater chance for success, so I will help them take full advantage of the opportunities and resources offered to them through this program.

CHAPTER 9

School Communications

QUESTION 9: HOW DO I STAY IN THE LOOP?

Extra, extra, read all about it. Parents want to know how to stay updated with all that's happening at school. So simply put, how can we keep up with so much? The short answer, know your options. I've discovered that most parents that are disconnected from school business are so because they aren't aware of the many sources available to them for information, or they have simply neglected to read what was shared. To stay in the loop, you have to know where to find the information. Let's take a look at common tools of communication and how each school level uses them.

Tools of Communication

School Website: Online source where you can find general information about the school including school leadership (administration), faculty and staff contact information, clubs & athletics specifics and sponsors, magnet programs/academies/school-wide initiatives, federal mandates, event calendars, numbers/addresses/school hours, lunch menus or links, registration and testing information, and etc.

Teachers may also have their own class pages that are linked here.

School Calendar: The school calendar is usually housed on the school's website. This is different from the district's calendar that gives information like first and last day of school, teacher planning days, and holidays & breaks. The school calendar highlights the dates noted on the district's calendar along with school specific activities like picture day, game days, parent meetings, school-wide celebrations, testing dates, club activities, and student deadlines. It is constantly updated as activities arise and should be pretty prominent on the school's website, as in one of the first things that you see.

Newsletters: Electronic or print updates on recent happenings at the school (or class) including upcoming meetings, events, school achievements, assignments, and activities requiring community input.

Portals: Website that contains information about grades, attendance, class assignments/projects and other specifics. You may also find school and district announcements here too. Most districts have both a student and parent portal. Student portals allow access to class webpages that teachers update with information on assignments and attachments/links to curriculum resources. The parent portal is used mainly as a way to monitor student academic progress. Some parent portals also house information on attendance, student balances (library, lunch, extracurricular activities), behavior, and access to teacher pages and contact information.

Robot Calls: Mass phone calls sent out to all families about school news, events, and updates including emergencies.

Text Reminders/Apps: Text message updates from the school sent to those families that have elected to receive them through a registration process. Text reminders are usually an opt-in service due to it being illegal to send unsolicited text messages to cell phones through an auto dialer system (ftc.gov 2013). Text messages as a form of communication is quickly becoming a parent's favorite with nearly 50% of parents in a recent survey preferring a text for information and only 19% wanting to go to the school's website for the same info (A.Rose March 2018). *Remind* is one of the more popular text reminder services used by schools.

Social Media: Facebook, Twitter, YouTube, and Instagram are popular channels schools now use to communicate with parents and families, but you only see the posting if you follow the page or user. It's wise to know that due to the many complex algorithms used by social media sites, you will only see postings from those pages and users that you engage with regularly. So if you want to see school postings, make sure to not only follow, but visit/like/comment on their posts so that you will see more of their information in the future. If you don't engage with their posts then the social media sites will take that as you not being interested in their content so they will show you less of it.

Agenda Books: Agenda books are like student planners. They work like calendars with space for students to record assignments such as homework, projects, and tests. Usually there is a space for parents to write a comment or sign. Teachers at the elementary level use agenda books as a way to communicate with parents by sending daily or weekly notes about the progress of the student in class and any concerns they may have. As the child gets older, the agenda books are used less and less as a parental communication tool with very little usage in middle school and pretty much zero usage in high school as a form of parent communication. Middle school agenda books have become more of an organizational tool than communication tool.

Behavior Charts: As with agenda books, behavior charts are more common at the lower levels. Behavior charts are ways that teachers communicate with families on the specifics of the child's daily behavior. A variety of systems exist including a stoplight system, a point system, smiling faces and frowns. The teacher will explain the system at the beginning of the year for clarity. The charts are a quick way to assess the day and provide quick feedback for the student and teacher.

Marquees: One of the oldest forms of school communication is the good ol' outdoor school signage or the marquee. We've become accustomed to seeing info on the most important school activities plastered on the traditional marquees with interchangeable letters, and now the upgraded electronic ones. However, space is limited so the information shared using this method will be too.

Email: By far, email is the parent's preferred choice for receiving information about their student. Emails can be general or personalized and are not restricted to the business hours of the school. This flexibility offers a greater chance to reach the desired audience and to get a response.

Postcards: Postcards are used for special occasions to highlight a specific activity or achievement. The idea is, who doesn't like to receive HAPPY MAIL? Most commonly used on the elementary level.

Letters: Once a standard source of communication is now usually reserved for information requiring a "paper trail." A paper trail, or additional tracking, may be a document that needs a signature as proof of receipt, verification of residency, a district communication, or etc.

Flyers/posters: A staple in our children's education is the faithful flyer with details advertising a particular event or offering like that upcoming fundraiser. Once upon a time all flyers were printed, but thanks to technology not anymore. More and more schools are moving toward electronic flyers as a means to be eco-friendly or "green" and also a way to save money (the other green).

Weekly Folders: Weekly folders are very common in elementary school.. The weekly folder houses graded papers, newsletters, school flyers, and grade/behavior reports. It's as close to one-stop shopping as you can get when it comes to school news. Sadly this practice disappears by the time the student reaches middle school as the focus switches from the parent's accountability to the student's accountability.

Communication Practices at Each Level

Now that we understand the tools commonly used in school for communication, what can we expect to see at each school level?

Elementary School

The students are young, their focus is usually short, and they are just now becoming comfortable with articulation of information. For these reasons and more, much of what's communicated to the homes at the elementary level is done so directly with the parents. Expect lots of hard copies of information including student work samples/graded work, flyers, grade reports, behavior reports, newsletters, and permission slips. There is still a great shuffle of papers at the elementary level. Also expect to communicate with the teacher through agenda books as well as via email. Text services are not as popular at this level, but give it some time. Phone calls are still expected in elementary school as the teachers usually have way fewer students than at the middle and high level making it a little easier to personally phone them (compare calling 30 parents to 150+). School websites are helpful and usually reiterate the information that's communicated in the weekly folder along with school basics. The school website becomes more relevant when the weekly folders are not an option.

Middle School

The kids are older, more accustomed to the school flow and expectations, and able to better articulate what they want and need. At this level, we begin to see a shift of responsibility from the parent to the student. Communications in middle school is more technology dependent and the absence of hard copies becomes apparent. Those phone calls that you have learned to expect may become far and few as teachers now have vastly more parents to communicate with, and are seeking more efficient ways to do so. Because of this, most have turned to emails and text reminders. If you are someone scared of technology, you may want to take a class as that will be your go to for keeping up. Now that weekly folders are out, the school's website is of more relevance and the place to go for regular announcements and updates. Newsletters are hit or miss at this level and really dependent on the culture of the school. If you are on social media, be sure to follow all the school pages as quick updates will show up there faster than the website. If you begin to feel out the loop a little, it's okay. The shift is happening. Teachers are communicating more directly with students and expecting students to begin advocating for themselves versus parents speaking on their behalf. Therefore they will still communicate with you regularly, but don't be surprised if it's more so as a general group than individually. When it is time to reach you personally, they will. The seriousness and urgency of the matter (good or bad) will determine if an email or phone call is necessary as initial contact and if an one on one meeting is needed as a follow-up.

High School

"We never hear from the teachers," is a common cry from parents at this level, and it's partly true. You will hear from the high school, BUT it will be way less than previous levels. The expectation at this stage is student accountability and less parent responsibility. By this point, students have matured (somewhat) and are well able to speak on their behalf. Therefore teachers are communicating directly with them, the student, as preparation for the independence needed after graduation. HOWEVER, they are still supplying information we can use. In high school, the school's website is a gold mine with resources on course selections, credits, postgraduation options, along with event calendars and fyi on class dues, responsibilities, clubs and athletics. Like middle school, you will find that high schools depend on technology for much of their communication. Paper communications at this point are almost a thing of the past. Check your email often as this is the option of choice for direct communication from teachers, club sponsors, and athletic program leaders. I've also discovered that text reminders and social media are more popular amongst the high school crowd as school officials are looking for ways to incorporate one of the most popular technological devices, our smartphones.

The Elephant in the Room: Grades

From over a decade of working with families in education, I have concluded that the best way to monitor a student's academic progress is with a weekly check. I have watched countless parents suffer complete overwhelm and frustration by existing on polar ends of the monitoring spectrum. I've had parents that wanted grade updates all the time and would email the teacher or check the gradebook DAILY! I've also had parents that would completely ignore their child's academic progress until the very end of the grading period or when alerted to areas of academic concern. Both methods caused unnecessary stress on all parties involved. Thanks to gradebook/parent portals, an online 24-7 option to staying on top of a student's academic progress, there is no need to stalk the teacher or be a disengaged parent. How your child is progressing in school is literally a login away. If you have not registered for this service, make it a priority. The process is simple and normally can be done fully online or with a short visit to the school. Gradebooks go by many different names and when in doubt, visit the *district's website* and look for the parent tab to find what it's called and how to access it. Schools will have the info on their sites too. After reviewing hundreds of school and district websites, I've just found the info was easier to locate on the district's site. We work smarter not harder. Don't forget that there is always a school representative that can show you how to navigate the gradebook system, be it a teacher or delegated parent support personnel. A phone call to the front office will get you connected with the right individual.

Why a weekly check? I am a fan of a weekly check because I've been in the classroom as a teacher, and I know that assignments aren't graded instantly. Just because the homework was due today or the test was taken today, does not mean the grade will be in the gradebook today. Teachers have many tasks that they are juggling and need to be given the proper time to manage them. It is common for grades to be updated weekly ;therefore, if you monitor grades weekly, you can stay up to date on the progress being made in class and any additional supports needed. There is not a particular day to choose. Pick what works best for your schedule. The key is to be consistent. Consistency keeps all parties from venturing on rescue missions and offers opportunities for timely celebration of a job well done.

-----Messenger Tips-----

- Review the school calendar early in the year and mark important dates on your own calendar.

- Visit the school's website the same day you check grades. This way you are updated on academic progress and school happenings.

- Pay attention to teacher emails and text reminders. Urgent information regarding class is usually communicated using these means.

- Find out how the school communicates last minute information like bus delays, inclement weather issues, and emergencies. Make sure you subscribe to all the services they use to communicate that information, including social media.

- Make sure the child is invested in the communication and update process too. They should also know how to stay up to date on occurrences at school, how to locate assignments, teacher pages, resources, and grades. The older the child is, the more responsible they are for this information. To help in the beginning, you can review information together.

- By high school, we are not emailing the teacher on a regular to talk about how the student is doing. The student should be advocating for themselves by this point. Check gradebook regularly and converse with the student often.

- Speak to your child about school on a regular basis. Ask questions like, how do they think they're doing? What are they absolutely rocking and where are they struggling? Never forget that your child is a great source of information as they are the *main* participatory party. They are the students.

I WILL HELP MY KID DOMINATE THE SCHOOL YEAR WITHOUT LOSING IT BY...

Knowing my options for school communications and staying in the loop through regular update checks. I will be consistent in monitoring grades, attendance, teacher communications, and school activities through the use of gradebook, the school website, and other offered services. I will be proactive with communications and monitoring as online resources are now available 24-7, and I will help my child be proactive too. Those that know can grow, and I will help my kid dominate the school year by staying in the know.

CHAPTER 10

Extracurricular and Enrichment Activities

QUESTION 10: WHAT OPPORTUNITIES ARE AVAILABLE AT THE SCHOOL?

Parents are deeply concerned about the academic rigor of the school. They want to make sure the student is receiving a *good education*, aka "the work is challenging and exposes them to the necessary skills needed to be successful in the future." But many are also interested in the opportunities to further develop a gift or talent the student has outside the classroom as well. For this reason, I am often asked, "What after-school activities, clubs, or sports does the school have?" Allow me to shed some light on this topic..

Extracurricular and Enrichment Activities

The offerings of extracurricular and enrichment activities at a school will vary based on the location of the school, demographics of population served, access to funding, and available leadership. The activities of a school in Alaska may vary greatly from that of one in Hawaii. There is no one size fits all list. What we do have are standards. At every level, elementary through high school, you will generally find student government, clubs representing the fine arts, sports (whether interscholastic or intramural), mentoring groups, service organizations, academic competitive teams, before and after school programs, tutoring, and special interest groups. The best place to look to see what is available at your child's school is the school's website. There should be a "student" tab or link to quickly access this information. Specific club and athletic information is most likely found there too. A second source of information is the school's counselor. The counselors are well aware of the many offerings of the school and the community. It is part of their responsibility to recommend programs and services to students and families as options for social-emotional growth and personal development. Another go to for info would be the parent and family support personnel at the school. This is the person mainly responsible for family engagement and community outreach activities. This person may be easier to locate in Title I schools than non-Title I Schools, but all schools should have staff responsible for this task. Now, once you've found the options and you need specifics, contact the coach or sponsor associated with the group. They will be the best qualified to answer questions on structure, membership, try-outs, dues, mandatory dates, & etc.

What We Know about the "Extras"

The argument for participating in extracurricular activities is strong and goes back decades. It is believed that extracurricular activities offer a means for students to express and explore their identity in challenging settings outside of academics. Here's what the research says about it:

1. Participation in extracurricular activities, even those not obviously associated with academic achievement, leads to increased commitment to school and school values, which leads indirectly to increased academic success. (Marsh ,1992)

2. Involvement in extracurricular activities also helps at-risk students. John Mahoney and Robert Cairns (1997) indicated that engagement in school extracurricular activities is linked to decreasing rates of early school dropouts in both boys and girls.

3. Participating in extracurricular activities helps adolescents come to understand themselves by observing and interpreting their own behavior when they are engaged in these activities (Valentine, Cooper, Bettencourt, & DuBois, 2002).

4. In addition to the developmental tasks that are fulfilled, researchers have posited that participation in extracurricular activities affords adolescents the op-

portunity to develop social capital in the form of extended supportive networks of friends and adults (McNeal, 1999).

So, as you can see. There is evidence that speaks to the link between extracurricular activities and academic achievement, relationship building, character strengthening, and soft skills. We know as parents that all children are not academic scholars. That doesn't mean they aren't intelligent. It just means based on the current criteria used in schools to measure academic excellence, they are not at the top of the food chain. The facts found in much of the aforementioned research remind us how sports, clubs, and performance groups can offer other opportunities for our kids to shine. Accomplishments boost the ego. They do. And sometimes that extra push of feeling good is all you need to help you grow as a whole and perform better in other areas. Plus, can we talk about how stressful school is? The testing craze has changed the culture of so many schools that our children often don't have a chance to just relax, to be silly, to act like kids while engaging with the content. Extracurricular activities create an outlet to interact with your peers and teachers away from the traditional academic environment. During this time, the students are more at ease and so are the adults. As a result, there is a greater chance of making a true connection. I've seen kids that many considered problematic show the most restraint and make the best grades in classes taught by their coaches or club sponsors. It wasn't because the adults were "giving them A's." It was because there was a relationship in place, mutual respect, and now the expectations of the teacher made sense.

The "Extras" and the Next Level

When applying for jobs, most companies require a resume. They want to quickly assess your skills, character, and track record of excellence. The same goes for college and other post-graduation options. While a resume or portfolio is not required everywhere, our kids will be asked to provide a transcript, test scores, and proof of school involvement, leadership, and community service. Selection committees nowadays are looking for the "total package." They want students at their institutions that are well-rounded, risk-takers, and can adapt to multiple environments. They want kids that are aware of the world and their role in it. Gone are the days of a great GPA alone swooning the masses. These days you must show versatility and evidence of time management along with academic achievement. In walks…extracurricular activities. Yes, through these activities our kids are gaining soft skills like communication, leadership, empathy, negotiation, and problem solving, but they are also building their "resume." A student that applies for a scholarship with a 3.8 and high test scores may be considered a good candidate. But the student that applies with a 3.5, slightly lower test scores, played sports, held leadership positions in multiple school clubs, did ongoing community service, and placed in the county science fair would be an even better selection. Yes, their GPA and test scores are lower, but the "extras" show that they have great time management skills and were still able to show academic achievement in the classroom while being a part of multiple ventures. Remember parents, we are helping our kids build skills, but we are also helping them build their "resume" for the next level.

-----Messenger Tips-----

- Go over extracurricular and enrichment opportunities with your child. Let them decide in which activities to participate. Look for a mix. Not all sports, not all fine arts, or academic enrichment, but a variety. There's nothing wrong with you encouraging them to try something out of their comfort zone too.

- DON'T OVER SCHEDULE YOUR KID. We all need downtime. Having kids in too many activities can do more harm than having them in none at all. If your child has no days off, that's a potential problem. Talk to them about the load they're carrying. Check their interest level. Make sure the activity is still a joy and not a burden. There may be some trying periods, but if the activity is looking more like a task than a joy, it might be time to revisit the decision. The "extras" are not forms of punishment.

- Monitor grades along with participation. These enrichment activities should NOT take away from the child's academic performance in class. They should enhance not distract. If you notice that grades are dropping or the child is failing a class, it's time to regroup! I've seen too many times when parents allowed the extras to take the lead. You'll find a star athlete that doesn't graduate. Nonsense! These activities are called EXTRAcurricular for a reason. They are never more important than the coursework.

- Be ALL IN. Once the decision is made to participate, plan to do it and do it well. Show up to practices, meetings, games, and concerts. Remind your child that hard work pays off and commence to being their biggest cheerleader.

I WILL HELP MY KID DOMINATE THE SCHOOL YEAR WITHOUT LOSING IT BY...

Seeking out opportunities for them to grow through extracurricular activities. I realize academic adeptness is not enough and opportunities for social, emotional, relational, and physical growth may be found in these enrichment activities. I plan to support my child's success through exposure to variety thus building their "resume" for greater post-graduation possibilities.

CHAPTER 11

School Topics Gone Viral

QUESTIONS 11: WHAT ARE SCHOOLS DOING ABOUT BULLYING?

Bullying has existed probably as long as people have. I can picture Eve bullying Adam in the Garden of Eden right now. No, but seriously it's been around forever and most associate it with grade school kids as a coming of age grade school behavior (It's most popular in middle school). So, why all the talk now? Why is bullying a school topic gone viral and forever trending? For starters, this ain't your mama's bullying. The bullying of today has gone past the stealing of lunch money or mean girl snarky comments. The bullying of today has gone past the "What Are Those???" clothes and shoes comments. Today smartphones record pretty much everything and a once "only a few people know about it; let me figure out how to handle this" occurrence has turned into a viral sensation. From my parenting circles, I have gathered that many adults feel kids have become desensitized. Pain inflicted on another person has become entertainment available on any device with a screen, so when it happens in real life the reaction to it is often no reaction at all. Unless you are the victim of course. So what are schools doing about it?

How are they handling bullying? For starters, let's get a working definition of *bullying*. According to the American Psychological Association (APA):

> **Bullying** is a form of aggressive behavior in which someone intentionally and repeatedly causes another person injury or discomfort. Bullying can take the form of physical contact, words or more subtle actions. The bullied individual typically has trouble defending him or herself and does nothing to "cause" the bullying(American Psychological Association, 2018).

A key word in the definition is "repeatedly." A one-time incident usually does not constitute bullying. Bullying is the presence of a repeated behavior. We must keep this in mind when discussing the topic with our children and school officials.

Now because we are well into the millennium and access to the internet and social media is available 24/7, we must too consider the idea of an evolved form of bullying, **cyberbullying**. "The same qualities of repeated, intentional, and social/psychological power plays are involved with cyberbullying. The only difference is that the bullying takes place via electronic mediums such as cell phones, computers, or other electronic devices" (Cyberbullying, 2018). So essentially, cyberbullying is done exclusively online in the verbal or visual form whereas your traditional bullying can be physical. In terms of cyberbullying, think threatening or condemning text messages, emails, and social media posts. Also, remember that it is much easier for the bully to hide their identity with cyberbullying as they may remain anonymous through non-disclosure contact information or fake social media accounts.

What are schools doing about it? For starters, there is more open dialogue about what it is and isn't. Bullying is a term loosely used, and it's very important that people know the difference between a disagreement, an unpleasant remark, a fight, and bullying because they are not all the same. By shedding light on the differences, you can decrease the number of false reportings to focus on the real issues at hand. Schools are also reinforcing the chain of command. They want students to know who to speak to and when. The numbers were all over the place when it came to research, but the message was clear. Most bullied students don't report it. They don't tell. There's been a slight increase in this area over the years, but it's definitely not enough. Schools are discussing with students their reporting options which are pretty unlimited and begin with them speaking with a trusted adult about the situation, usually a favorite teacher or the counselor. Bullying resolution methods are commonly handled at the counselor's office as bullying affects more than just academic achievement, but also social, emotional, and mental health. Some of the resolution methods outside of reporting it include simply ignoring it, confronting the aggressor, removing yourself from potential meetups, increasing partner and group activities so you are not alone, joining clubs/sports teams/classes to boost your confidence and self-esteem to name a few. Another strategy being used is peer intervention. It is said that acts of bullying stop within 10 seconds when bystanders intervene (American SPCC, n.d., para 7). Schools all over are stressing to students to not be passive spectators. Schools would rather students to stop the bullying or report it. Stopping it may involve telling the bully to change their behavior or removing the bullied from the situation by walking away with them. There are many anti-bullying initiatives with videos of celebrities encouraging kids to stand up and take action against bullying, and it appears that kids are listening. Here's a closer look at what schools are and can do about bullying taken from a 2018 CDC Report:

- *Multi-tiered systems of support,* which includes universal programs or activities for all youth within the community or school; selective interventions for groups of youth at risk for being involved in bullying; and preventive interventions tailored for students already involved in bullying.

- *Multicomponent programs* that address multiple aspects of bullying behavior and the environments that support it. Examples include examining school rules and using behavior management techniques and social emotional learning in the classroom and throughout the school to detect and provide consequences for bullying.

- *School-wide prevention activities* that include improving the school climate, strengthening supervision of students, and having a school-wide anti-bullying policy.

- *Involving families and communities* by helping caregivers learn how to talk about bullying and get involved with school-based prevention efforts.

- *Developing long-term school-wide approaches* that strengthen youth's social-emotional, communication, and problem-solving skills.

- *Focusing on program fidelity* by forming an implementation team to make sure the programs are carried out exactly as they were designed.

What most excites me about the list are two things: the focus on school climate and families and communities. Bullies love attention and usually engage in aggressive acts for the approval of an audience or the power gained from others watching or knowing of their acts. When schools work on culture and climate, they have the ability to remove the "fans." So many people are interested in going "viral" even if for something negative. If you take the watchers and recorders away, they are less likely to engage in the activity. You can only have a viral video if someone records what you're doing. Many schools are promoting tolerance of differences and unity and allowing students to have a greater say in programming, decision making, and student expression. This "we're all in this together" approach creates a climate of acceptance and tolerance which makes those showing behaviors other than these *outsiders*. As for parents and communities, schools are aware that bullying is not limited to the school and therefore can't be fully rectified at the school. The school has a primary focus on student learning We need parents and the communities to provide resources for the social, emotional, and mental health gaps that are most likely present in students being bullied and the actual bully. If multiple parties are a part of the solution, then bullying is no longer looked at as a problem the *schools* have, but as a problem the *community* has. Because honestly, it's just that. Kids, while they may be influenced, don't morph into different beings at school. Who they are when they leave our house is who they are when they enter the school---even if they take on the role of the bullied or the bully. So the community and parents have ownership of this issue too, and we are reminded of it more and more with every news report of a youth suicide or school shooting.

No doubt that news reports or raving reviews for Netflix's *13 Reasons Why* have us all looking at bullying and the rising number of youth suicides more and more. It would be unwise for us to not think there is a connection, but it would be just as unwise for us to think bullying is the only reason youth suicide is on the rise. That's a completely different topic that we will dive into at another time, but for now....school shootings.

QUESTION 12: WHAT ARE SCHOOLS DOING ABOUT SCHOOL SHOOTINGS/SAFETY?

Truth be told, most schools began actively preparing for school shootings after the Columbine Massacre of 1999. That incident was a wake-up call to just how vulnerable schools were and the beginning of school "lockdowns." A school "lockdown" is essentially just that, the locking of the school. A lockdown usually consist of the announcing of the lockdown, the locking of exits, offices, and classrooms, staff guiding students away from windows and out of sight of danger. The idea is to keep students controlled by keeping them confined to a specific area with adult supervision. This way, staff can account for who is in the building and speak confidently about their condition.

Other safety measures schools are taking include double entries, metal detectors, armed resource officers (police), armed staff, greater social media vigilance, town hall resource meetings, and more access to mental health services.

Double Entries

All schools in my district received security updates to entrances over the summer. Before you could simply walk through the door, and you were in a common area of the school with access to students and staff. Now you have to enter the first set of doors (often you have to be buzzed in) to a restricted access area. At this point, it is you and limited office staff. You do not have access to any common areas. After you have been vetted, you may then carry on the business for your visit and will gain entry to the main areas of the school. And all of these actions are caught on camera of course.

Metal Detectors

One of the most commonly known school safety measures is the metal detector. The idea is simple. Everyone that enters the school must go through the detector to check for weapons. Many schools use them, especially high schools. The problem with metal detectors is the cost. So many schools can't afford them or the updates and maintenance that they require.

Armed Resource Officers and Staff

Police officers, or resource officers, at school is no longer strange but common. The presence of an officer in uniform helps create a feeling of security. Most parents I speak to prefer a police officer to a security guard because the police officer has a greater presence of authority and more abilities and authority under the law. The addition of armed staff is new and not an idea embraced by the majority to whom I've spoken. The concern is if teachers have guns, there are more guns in schools and an even greater chance for them to fall in the wrong hands.

Greater Social Media Vigilance

Schools have begun to invest personnel and partner with the authorities to monitor social media happenings and investigate "concerns." It is no secret that social media has been very instrumental in providing probable cause to recent shootings and stopping others from occurring. The reasoning here is if we can stay on top of it, we can prevent it. Students are using social media to communicate constantly. If we want to know what they are discussing and sharing, we must use it too.

Town Hall Meetings

School shootings aren't just a school problem; it's a community problem. Mass shootings as a whole are problematic in this country. Schools are now taking greater strides to work with parents and the community to create safer schools and hence, safer communities. Town hall meetings are opportunities for stakeholders to come together to educate each other on the matter and discuss viable solutions to the problem. It's a meeting of the minds to pull together to see how WE, not the school, but all of us, can fix what affects so many. I had a chance to attend a student school safety town hall meeting in 2018 sponsored by Kids on the Move for Success, Dekalb County Public Schools, and the Dekalb County Police Department. I left the meeting so impressed and optimistic. The true idea of partnership was exemplified. Not only were the adults discussing the issue of school safety, but the kids were too and as equal partners. Often the grownups meet to discuss solutions and form a plan of action. This time the students were able to lead many discussions and their views were heard and respected. When it comes to school safety, we cannot afford to have conversations on how to bring it to past without those directly affected, the students and families.

Mental Health Services

School counselors are a great source of knowledge when it comes to student behaviors and mental health. Many schools are increasing the counseling capabilities of the staff through trainings and schoolwide program adoption. Another move being made is the increase of partnerships with organizations that service the community outside the school to offer what is known in education as wraparound services. The school is simply not capable of handling all student issues effectively because it was designed to focus on academic achievement. We must drop the expectation of schools to be a jack of all trades. It is unfair and unrealistic. Many services must be outsourced to those specifically trained and properly staffed to handle such cases. Mental health education is becoming more in demand (time consuming) and requires the assistance of organizations that specialize in this field. Bringing in additional resources to support the school's safety endeavors is becoming a hot topic amongst legislatures, and we should expect the arrival of new bills to support their efforts soon (Loftus and McLaren, 2019).

If I had to predict the future, I would say that bullying and school shootings and safety will continue to be trending topics. Considering 2018 was the worst year on record for school gun violence with 96 reported incidences and 56 deaths, we can be sure the discussion won't be going away anytime soon (US Naval Postgraduate School, 2018). There is still so much work to do, but we can be confident in knowing the work has started.

------Messenger Tips-----

How WE Can Help

- Stay in the loop! Attend meetings (live or webinars) that discuss the issues and actively participate.
- Build a relationship with your child that allows them to be HEARD. So often parents do the talking. Make sure your child knows that they can speak to you about anything WITHOUT JUDGEMENT. If we continue to dissect what they say for opportunities to show how we are right, they will stop talking. How can they tell us about being bullied if they feel they can't come to us? Remember, most kids don't tell. We need ours to be the exception.
- Probe. Ask your child specific questions about bullying and note their responses AND their body language. Often actions speak louder than words.
- Have access to all online accounts, social media included. This is not us invading their space. This is a

matter of us keeping them safe, and it is absolutely necessary. Once you have access, periodically check. Let your child know that you won't stalk them, but you will occasionally check. We don't want to be the parent on the news crying saying "I didn't know" after pages of Snapchat and Instagram posts were filled with clues.

- Watch for sudden changes in behavior, grades, health, injuries, and attendance. Students bullied are prone to miss school to avoid the bully (they will even fake an illness).

- Make sure your child has contact information for at least 3 people to call in case of an emergency. They should know these numbers by memory.

- Watch for aggressive and violent language, behavior, and the sudden attainment of "trinkets" (money, attire, electronics, etc.). Bullies have parents too, and we need to address our children if they are the bully.

- Openly discuss bullying with the child. Discuss what it is, how it may look (physical and online), how it may feel, what to do if they see it happening (report it), what the consequences are for doing it. Sometimes bullying becomes a criminal activity and is punishable by jail time and more. Many kids don't know this.

- Review the school's handbook on how they define and address bullying and school safety. This information should be available as a hard copy or online on the school or district's website.

I WILL HELP MY KID DOMINATE THE SCHOOL YEAR WITHOUT LOSING IT BY...

Staying in the loop in regards to hot topics like bullying and school safety. I will familiarize myself and my child with the school's procedure for handling such issues. I will also become an active participant in developing solutions to the problems by participating in school functions that speak to those issues, and I will allow my child to have a voice to do the same. I will constantly speak positivity over my child to remind them of their abilities and value. We, as a family, will not become victims of fear, but optimistic problem solvers and school supporters.

CHAPTER 12

Testing

QUESTION 13: WHAT IS GOING ON WITH ALL THIS TESTING?

Testing, testing, testing, and yet more testing. By this point, I'm sure you've heard about all the testing that today's students are responsible for taking. It's hard to miss. There are constant reminders about testing on the school's website, in newsletters, emails, and even on the news. And even though we hear about testing all the time, I'm constantly asked by parents "What and why?" Well to understand where we are currently in this testing era, we have to go back to 2001 and the start of No Child Left Behind.

The Past

Students taking test to measure academic progression is not a new concept, and it existed long before 2001. However, what happened in 2001 was important to our education system in America because it promoted a reform system that tied academic progress to funding, teacher and staff retention, school choice, and offered a public report card of sorts to broadcast exactly how public schools everywhere were performing (A Parent's Handbook, 2011). This education system reform, good people, is known as no other than the No Child Left Behind Act (NCLB) which essentially was a rework of the 1965 Elementary and Secondary Education Act (ESEA). I believe the ideas of NCLB in many cases were admirable. Wanting the country to have a way to measure the progress of public education through a set of national standards could truly be beneficial to the improvement of education across the nation. Although, in my opinion, the amount of pressure brought on the schools to make adequate yearly progress made the initiative more of a negative than a positive. Under NCLB, every public school student in the nation would be tested in math and in reading or language arts each year in grades 3-8 and at least once during grades 10-12 (A Parent's Handbook, 2011). In walks the standardized testing frenzy. Once upon a time if you told a teacher they were "teaching to the test," those were fighting words. How dare you? Now if you say it, most will agree that's exactly what we do.

The Present

Fast forward to 2018 and NCLB no longer exists. It has been replaced with the Every Student Succeeds Act of 2015 (ESSA) which is another attempt at national education reform, but it gives more decision making power to the states thus weakening what many believed to be federal interference. Though NCLB is gone, standardized testing is not.

States all across the country continue to administer them. When schools speak consistently of "testing" it is usually the state mandated test that they are referencing. However, there is a snowball effect here. Districts all over began to panic over making the mark and necessary progress on standardized test so much that they began to initiate even more testing in the form of district benchmark assessments. These benchmark assessments are basically the districts' standardized tests. It's a way for each district to see how the students are learning and which areas need attention before students take the state standardized assessments. These tests are in addition to the quizzes, chapter, and unit tests that students take on a regular basis to measure skill and standard mastery attainment. Sounds like a lot of testing? I won't sugarcoat it for you. It is.

The Future

What does the future hold for testing? For one, it's not going away. How test are administered and how many are given will definitely change. It simply has to. The amount of parents, students, and educators dissatisfied with the amount and administering of testing is too many to ignore. According to a National Education Association (NEA) survey, 45% of teachers have considered leaving the profession due to standardized testing (Walker, 2014). That is almost half of those surveyed and considering my conversations with colleagues, that's about right. So what is being done? The feder-

127

al government is aware of the need to assess academic growth of students and holding schools accountable, but they are also aware of this growing epidemic of dissatisfaction. Due to this, there is an Innovative Assessment pilot program going on where states get to consider alternatives to the state standardized testing (Tagami, 2018). These alternatives can lead to less testing in schools. Georgia is one of the states that applied for the pilot program, and I couldn't be prouder of my state. Go Georgia!

What Parents Need to Understand

As parents, we need to understand that testing is a part of life. It's a measuring tool for acquired knowledge, and it won't stop at the conclusion of high school. Depending on the career path of an individual, testing may be needed for licensing or certification for jobs. This we must communicate with our children, but we do have the right to voice our concern and solutions to how tests are administered, the amount, and frequency at the school level.

An additional right parents have is that of the opt-out. Parents have the right to legally opt-out of testing for their children. That's right. Parents can say NO to standardized state testing for their kids (Strauss, 2018). I've been in education for over 14 years, and the first time I heard of the ability to opt-out of standardized state testing was from a parent four years ago. The parent was from Colorado and spoke of the growing opt-out movement out west. I was in disbelief and had to do research of my own. Who knew? It definitely was not something that was discussed within the school systems where I worked or my peers, yet it was true. I couldn't help but to think how many other parents were not aware of this right. Do your research to find out what is necessary of documentation for your school. Also keep in mind that private and charter adhere to different guidelines and may have a "no-opt out" testing policy that you must agree to prior to student enrollment. If this policy exists and you agreed to it in August, you can't turn around in April to say you changed your mind. It was a condition of the student's acceptance into the program. Sorry.

Another thing we need to understand as parents is preparation. How are the schools preparing our children for testing and how can we help? Every state has a set of core standards from which the curriculum is developed. The standards aren't necessarily the Common Core standards that are often mentioned in the news, but they are a set of basics that students must learn to show adequate knowledge in a subject area. Teachers use these standards daily for class instruction. These standards are later assessed with quizzes, chapter tests, unit tests, benchmarks, pretests, and ultimately the state standardized test. Our kids are exposed to the information that they will later be tested on and the various styles of testing questions (multiple choice, short response, and essay) prior to the test and often. As parents, we should know in which areas our kids will test and when. We should also be aware of strategies to share with our kids about testing. Honestly, testing strategies are everyday homework and classwork strategies. Things like: read the directions thoroughly; work out the problem before looking at the choices in math; read the question and options before reading the passage for reading or language arts; highlight, underline, or circle key words in the questions or passage are strategies that we should promote our children use *all the time* and not just during testing. It is important that we also not place too much stress on a test. Our children should understand that we do our best work at all times. A test is simply another opportunity to show what we know. When we make too big a deal out of tests, it communicates the message that other work done during the school year is not as critical. It also *shows* in our kids. I have experienced children shaking, vomiting, suffering panic attacks, and having bathroom "accidents" all because of testing. They were a nervous wreck! I've also witnessed kids that did fairly well in class completely fall to pieces during the test because of the pressure placed on them to excel. We must be careful with placing that much power on one assessment. There is plenty of research done to show what mental and emotional stress of testing does on those involved, but we have the ability to change the narrative.

Again, will testing go away? No. But we do have the ability to educate ourselves about them, voice our concern and solutions over them, prepare our children for them, and even opt-out of the state standardized test if necessary.

-----Messenger Tips-----

- Attend a parent "Test" meeting to learn about your local assessment, what the results mean for the student (pass, fail, is it used for promotion to the next grade), testing question format, practice aides, and testing options.

- If your student receives accommodations during the school year, check to see which accommodations will be allowed during testing. This is important to consider if your student is in the special education program or English as a Second Language (ESL) program.

- Teach children prone to anxiety breathing techniques.

- Focus on preparation throughout the school year and DO NOT CRAM in learning before a test. The last minute push to learn everything at once will increase the stress factor and may overwhelm the student and cause the adverse result, low test scores.

- Remind the student to do their best on a regular to establish the expectation of excellence thus making test day less stressful.

I WILL HELP MY KID DOMINATE THE SCHOOL YEAR WITHOUT LOSING IT BY...

Educating myself on standardized testing (and other testing) administered at the school. I will learn about which tests are given, when, and our options. I will help my student prepare for testing by making sure they focus on the work given throughout the school year. We will not participate in cram learning as that adds to the stress of the student and the parent. I will remind my student to do their best work at all times and this will translate to excellence every day including test day.

CLOSING

The Key to Their Success

Wouldn't it be great if kids came with a manual or a cheat sheet of sorts? Well, they don't. We have to navigate parenting the best way we can using the tools that we have. While difficult at times, it is truly one of the most rewarding jobs we will ever have. And make no doubt about it, it is work. It is our work. It is the work that we were hand selected to do. It's a job that no one else in the universe is qualified for because it was assigned to us from the very beginning. Now, let us find peace in knowing that if we were given the job to do, we were also equipped with the ability to do it successfully. See, the key to our children's success is a complex answer and family is critical.

As a classroom teacher of over 10 years, I had the opportunity to discover patterns. I discovered patterns of behavior, motivation, and of success in my students. What I noticed actually surprised me. While in school, I was told the most intellectually inclined would ultimately be the most successful. That was wrong. That was...wrong. While teaching, I discovered that the children that performed the best in my class were the ones that had the most parental and family backing. Hands down they represented the majority of my success stories. They weren't necessarily the students with the highest IQs or the highest standardized test scores. They weren't always the ones placed in the gifted program or on the accelerated track. By far, the most well-rounded and academically progressive students in the room were the ones with the strongest *family engagement*. It's basically the partnering of the families, schools, and communities for the successful development of the child which leads to stronger families, schools, and communities in return. The support system of the family was so strong that it made it impossible for the child to fail. And the child understood the expectations. Not just mine as the classroom teacher, but of their parents, their grandparents, their uncles, their aunties, and their big brother and sister. They knew that they were an extension of a rooted tree. Because of this knowledge, this support, there was visible intrinsic motivation on the child's part. There was an inner drive that made them want to work harder and do better. It was pride, it was hope, it was understanding, it was both motivating and motivational. And I loved to see them win. It was a true display of hard work and teamwork at its finest. The village earned the victory. That's why now I know. The research shows it, yes. But I've witnessed with my own eyes that one major key to a student's success is ultimately support through *family engagement*. "Family engagement is a shared responsibility in which schools and other community agencies and organizations are committed to reaching out to engage families in meaningful ways and in which families are committed to actively supporting their children's learning and development" (NAFSCE Policy Council, 2010). Ability is great, and we all have it. We all have the ability to do wondrous things, but we all don't. The difference usually comes in support. No one makes it to the top alone. There are no solo made success stories. We need each other, and when it comes to students, they need the support of the family. Parental involvement in a child's life is a greater indicator of success than any test created and any technology imaginable. What is interesting is that you can replace the word "parental" with "family" and get pretty much the same results. When the people that love you most are involved in the education process, stability is established and doors open. Students are free to learn, to fail, to get back up and try again because there is a trusted hand to help them do it.

QUESTION 14: AM I DOING ENOUGH?

You've made it to the end of this book. A book that you invested your time, money, and energy into in an effort to improve your child's chances of school success. You could have done anything else with those resources, but you decided to invest them here because this was important to you. If you are that type of parent, I'm pretty sure you are doing enough. But if you have any doubt, here's one way to double check. Project Appleseed Organization identifies what they call the 6 Slices of Parental Involvement when working with schools and communities for student success. The six slices are parenting, volunteering, learning at home, decision making, and collaborating with the community (Project Appleseed.org, 1996). All six "slices" were discussed in multiple ways throughout this book as tools for student success. Now it's time to be consistent. We have to establish healthy habits for true results. Follow the steps given within these pages. Try the strategies. Practice doesn't guarantee perfect, but it does guarantee better. Once we are consistent, progress will happen. We will be able to see the fruits of our labor and in our children the fruits of theirs. Obstacles will come. No problem. We can breathe, adjust, and get back on track. Remember that we are never alone as there are plenty of people at the school there to support us, so don't be afraid to ask for help. We are in this together and together we can do more than... enough.

So as we bring this journey to a close, I want you to reflect on the questions answered and the pledges made. Each answer to the burning questions involved you. You are a huge piece to this puzzle. Now, I challenge you to apply what you've learned from our time together to help your kid dominate not only this school year, but every school year. This is not the end but the beginning, because now you have been officially *schooled.*

ACKNOWLEDGEMENTS

From the heart comes much

I never in life thought that I would be an educator. My goal after college was to land a job at Hallmark writing content for greeting cards. Ha! The jokes on me. Just another example of what happens when you let go and let God.

A round of applause for Karen Mapp, Anne Henderson, Steve Constantino, NAFSCE, IEL, and the Global Family Research Project. You are the trailblazers of the family engagement movement and the source of much of our knowledge. I am so grateful for you and the opportunity to become "The School Messenger" by taking what we know as practitioners and simplifying it for understanding and application for our families. It looks like the country is finally taking notice of our work. Well it's about time!

Now for the man that gave me the green light to let loose and develop a family and community engagement program that would serve all our Shiloh Middle families, Dr. Eli Welch III. I could not have asked for a more flexible and encouraging school leader. These words are not commonly used by employees to describe their former bosses. There is NO WAY that I could have mustered the courage to spread my wings to impact as many families as possible without your blessing. From the very beginning, you saw my heart and understood my mission-- maybe even more than I did. You are such a servant driven leader that encourages his flock, and I was truly blessed to flourish under your leadership. You are impacting the field of family engagement more than you know, and I can't wait for the world to hear about your family and community impact programs and strategies.

Shout out to Lathrop Elementary, Clayton County, and Gwinnett County parents! Never have I met such a lively and committed group! I know what the media and the data may say, and I'm telling you to stay strong the positive results are on the way. I thought some of you were employees because you were so invested. YOU made me look great! Much of what I learned about parents and for families came from our time together. I know first-hand how involved parents can change the trajectory of a child and much of that I learned from you. We'll forever be family.

Thanks to my book squad: Abir Hasan for the rockin' cover design; Genine Bonaby (editor), Charner Rodgers (co-editor); Renae Jones, Adria Horton, Kaneisha Harris, Kim Mims, and Oliva Ogle for proofing; Rasel Khondokar for formatting; and Carla Ogle, Lamont Jones, Keitha Alexander, Marshatta Harris, Jane Rodriguez, and Vameker Banks for laughs and motivation during the trying times. There were many.

Family and friends and supporters old and new, I appreciate you. How many people get to say that they do what they truly love? Because of you, I can. It is my hope that my work enlightens you and supports your family's growth. By the way, follow me on all social media @bishonnajones. Shameless, I know. But if you are a fan of mine, well you're not surprised. Love ya!

Last but not least, all praises go to thee above. Never will I be ashamed to say I'm your child and never will I be ungrateful of the many blessings bestowed upon me. Yes, I'm a sometimes hot mess work in progress. But you already knew that. You commanded me to get out there to share this information and to save families in my own unique way. I'm trying, and I hope you're proud. Thank You God!

REFERENCES

Chapter 1

Summer Learning Lost Statistics (And Tips to Promote Learning All Summer Long). (2015, April 15). Retrieved from https://www.oxfordlearning.com/summer-learning-loss-statistics/

Chapter 4

20 US Code 7801-Definitions (27). (2018). Retrieved from https://www.law.cornell.edu/uscode/text/20/7801

Giftedness Defined NSGT. (2018). Retrieved from https://www.nsgt.org/giftedness-defined/

Lee, Andrew.(n.d.). Individuals With Disabilities Education Act: What You Need to Know. Retrieved from https://www.understood.org/en/school-learning/your-childs-rights/basics-about-childs-rights/individuals-with-disabilities-education-act-idea-what-you-need-to-know

Chapter 5

The Glossary of Education Reform. (2013, August 29). Retrieved from https://www.edglossary.org/grade-point-average/

Chapter 6

Bowles, Nellie. (2018, October 26). The Digital Gap Between Rich and Poor Kids is Not What We Expected. Retrieved from https://www.nytimes.com/2018/10/26/style/digital-divide-screens-schools.html

Chapter 8

Clark, Laura. (2018, August 29). The Basics of Title I Schools. Retrieved from https://www.studentdebtrelief.us/student-loans/title-1-schools/

Every Student Succeeds Act (ESSA-Sect 1001). (2015). Retrieved from http://www.everystudentsucceedsact.org/title-1-

National Center for Education Statistics (NCES) Fast Facts. (2018). Retrieved from https://nces.ed.gov/fastfacts/display.asp?id=158

US Department of Education (Programs). (2018). Retrieved from https://www2.ed.gov/programs/titleiparta/index.html

Chapter 10

Mahoney, J., & Cairns, R. (1997). Do extracurricular activities protect against early school dropout? Developmental Psychology, 33(2), 241–253.

Marsh, H. (1992). Extracurricular activities: Beneficial extension of the traditional curriculum or subversion of academic goals? Journal of Educational Psychology, 84(4), 553–562.

McNeal Jr, R.B.. (1999). Participation in high school extracurricular activities: Investigating school effects. Social Science Quarterly. 80. 291-309.

Valentine, Jeffrey. (2002) Out-of-School Activities and Academic Achievement: The Mediating Role of Self-Beliefs, Educational Psychologist, 37:4, 245-256, DOI: 10.1207/S15326985EP3704_4

Chapter 11

American Society for the Positive Care of Children (American SPCC). (n.d.). Bullying Definitions, Statistics, and Risk Factors. Para 7. Retrieved from https://americanspcc.org/our-voice/bullying/statistics-and-information/

American Psychological Association (APA) Bullying. (2018). Retrieved from https://www.apa.org/topics/bullying/

Center for Disease Control Prevention (CDC). (2018). Bullying Research. Retrieved from https://www.cdc.gov/violenceprevention/youthviolence/bullyingresearch/index.html

Cyberbullying. (2018). Retrieved from
https://backgroundchecks.org/cyber-bullying-helping-the-
bullied-stopping-the-bullies.html

Loftus, Tom and McLaren, Mandy. (2019, January 7). School
safety bill will deal with counselors, security, but not guns.
Retrieved from https://www.courier-
journal.com/story/news/politics/2019/01/07/school-safety-
response-expected-during-kentucky-legislative-
session/2482323002/

US Naval Postgraduate School. (2018). K-12 School Shooting
Database. Retrieved from https://www.chds.us/ssdb/

Chapter 12

A Parent's Handbook: Help Your Child Prepare for Standardized
Tests in Middle School. (2011 edition). (2009). P.4. South
Deerfield, MA: Channing Bete

Strauss, Valerie. (2018, June 8). The bottom line on opting out of
high-stakes standardized tests. Retrieved from
https://www.washingtonpost.com/news/answer-
sheet/wp/2018/06/08/the-bottom-line-on-opting-out-of-
high-stakes-standardized-
tests/?noredirect=on&utm_term=.f7e570588734

Tagami, Ty. (2018, December 13). Georgia to seek federal waiver
from year-end, state standardized tests. Retrieved from
https://www.ajc.com/news/state--regional-education/georgia-

apply-for-federal-waiver-from-year-end-state-standardized-
tests/DIhQ2LiY65Vf2FsMbavgNI/?fbclid=IwAR190xXVSciy
BDN_DXcdsRNGRvurhy153myzhX7weBxwHDTfyu79Wn
7tXSU

Walker, Tim. (2014, November 2). NEA Survey: Nearly Half Of
Teachers Consider Leaving Profession Due to Standardized
Testing. Retrieved from http://neatoday.org/2014/11/02/nea-
survey-nearly-half-of-teachers-consider-leaving-profession-
due-to-standardized-testing-2/

Closing

NAFSCE Policy Council. (2010). Family Engagement Defined.
Retrieved from https://nafsce.org/page/definition

Project Appleseed. (1996). 6 Slices of Family (Parental) Involvement. Retrieved from
https://www.projectappleseed.org/sixstandards

About the Author

Bishonna Jones, *The School Messenger*, is a veteran educator, speaker, and author. Jones has worked with thousands on the topics of family engagement, personal development, education, community activism, and resource utilization. Recognized by the Georgia Department of Education and multiple institutions for contributions to advance family and community engagement, Jones continues to captivate audiences with her real, relevant, and results-oriented approach to speaking and training. Need someone to motivate your group? Visit www.bishonnajones.com for more information on the author, staff trainings, education consulting, speaking, parent workshops, resources, and media requests. Follow Bishonna on all social media at @bishonnajones.